**Clever ways to create gifts
from everything in your garden**

Lynn Brittney
www.irisbooks.co.uk

IRIS BOOKS
www.irisbooks.co.uk

Iris Books is based in London, UK and is an imprint of Write Publications Ltd.

Gifts From Your Garden ~ Bumper Edition

This edition published in 2022 by Iris Books, an imprint of Write Publications Ltd.,
London, United Kingdom.

www.irisbooks.co.uk

ISBN 978-1-907147-84-5
Copyright Iris Books 2022

The right of Lynn Brittney to be identified as the creator of this work has been asserted by her in accordance with the Copyright, Designs and Patents Act 1988. This publication is protected under the Copyright laws currently existing in every country throughout the world.

All rights reserved. No part of this publication may be reproduced, stored in or introduced into a retrieval system, or transmitted in any form or by any means (electronic, mechanical, photocopying, recording or otherwise) without the prior written permission of the publisher. Any person who does any unauthorised act in relation to this publication may be liable to criminal prosecution and civil claims for damages.

This book is sold subject to the condition that it shall not, by way of trade or otherwise, be lent, resold, hired out or otherwise circulated without the publisher's prior consent, in any form of binding or cover other than that in which it is published and without a similar condition including this condition being imposed on the subsequent purchaser.

Design by Kate Lowe
Printed in the United Kingdom.

Gifts from your Garden Bumper Edition

Contents

SECTION 1: *Culinary*

Teas or Tisanes	2
Fruit Cordials or Squashes	4
Bottled Fruit	6
Jam	10
Floral Syrups	13
Dried Fruits	14
Fruit Leathers	15
Infused Vinegars	17
Infused Oils	18
Dried Herb Parcels or Pots	20
Dried Peas and Beans	22
Nuts and Seeds	24
Pickles	26
Chutneys	28
The Ultimate Sauce	29
Savoury Dips	30
Making your own Mustards	31
Flavoured Butters and Cheeses	32

Disclaimer: Please note that all the recipes in this book are merely suggestions and can be adapted as the reader wishes. Please ascertain whether the person you are intending to present with an edible gift has any allergies. Please ensure that you label all edible gifts with date processed and instructions for storage and usage. Please endeavour to make sure that the edible gifts are freshly made when you gift them.

SECTION 2: *Health and Beauty*

Fruit Tonics	34
Footbaths	36
Cough Syrups	38
Steam Inhalations	40
Mouthwashes	42
Tooth Powder	44
Eye Health	45
Bath Salts	46
Bath Bombs	47
Hair Oils	48
Hair Rinses	50
Perfumed Salves	52
Looking after Hands & Feet	54
Nails	56
Lip Balms	57
Face Masks	58
Cheat's Liquid Soap	61
Insect Repellents	62

Disclaimer: Please note that all remedies and recipes in this book are merely suggestions and can be adapted as the reader wishes. Please ascertain whether the person you are intending to present with a gift made from plants has any allergies; is pregnant, or has small children in the house, Please ensure you label all your plant-based gifts with date processed and instructions for storage and usage.

SECTION 3: *Crafts*

Preserving Flowers and Foliage — 66

What can you create with Dried Flowers? — 69

Potpourri — 71

Pressed Flowers — 72

What can you make with Pressed Flowers? — 74

Seed Bomb, Balls, Mats and Tapes — 77

Indoor Gardens — 80

Making Gifts from Wood — 83

Dyes from your Plants — 86

Christmas — 88

Scented Gifts — 94

Disclaimer: Please note that all the crafts suggested in this book involve the use of glues, varnishes and other chemical substances. We hope that readers will take care when undertaking these tasks. Always wear protective clothing and gloves – also eye shields when drilling or sanding wood. Children should be supervised when undertaking craft work. Do not use spray glue or varnish when pets are in the room. Always do craft work in a well-ventilated room.

SECTION 4: *Treats*

Herbs for Cocktails and Mocktails	98
Using Edible Flowers in Drinks	99
A Berry Good Idea	102
Candies!	103
Ice Creams, Sorbets and Lollies	106
Stuffed, Fried and Dipped	110
Flower and Fruit Fritters	113
Party Nibbles	115
Cakes made from Veg	118
Fruit instead of Veg?	120
Jellies, Fools and Meringues	121

Disclaimer: Please note that all the recipes in this book are merely suggestions and can be adapted as the reader wishes. Please ascertain whether the person or persons that you are intending to present with an edible treat has any allergies. Please ensure that when you make treats for a party or gathering, that you inform people what ingredients have been used in the creation of those treats. There are some recipes which contain alcohol and therefore are not suitable for children.

Please note that some ingredients are toxic for animals (when in doubt check here: www.humanesociety.org/resources/foods-can-be-poisonous-pets) so keep such treats out of the reach of household pets.

SECTION 1 : *Culinary*

Teas or Tisanes

Technically, tea can only be made from actual tea leaves from the Camellia Sinensis plant, and naturally contains caffeine. Any hot drink made from another plant is a tisane or infusion, which should be caffeine free.

Obviously, there are some plants that should never be consumed, as they are poisonous or can cause health problems if drunk in any quantity. Therefore we suggest that you stick to the list we have provided here, or do your own research before using any plant as a tisane, that will be ingested.

Some plants need to be dried before using in tisanes, as the flavour is better. Other plants work just as well if the fresh leaves or flowers are used. If fresh leaves are used, bruise the leaves first, to release oils and use a small handful. With dried herbs, put a heaped teaspoonful in an infuser ball and hang it in the pot or cup, then pour over the hot water and allow to infuse. Add a small spoonful of honey to your cup if preferred.

Making Tisanes as Gifts

Opposite is a list of plants for making tisanes and a basic list of their benefits. However, many plants are said to have more than one benefit to the body, so we suggest that you research your chosen plants before electing to dry them to make tea sachets. The sachets could be muslin wraps or bags with a long string so that they can be hung in a small teapot or cup to brew. Label the teas carefully and provide the recipient with some explanation of the benefit of the tisanes you are gifting. Also make sure that the recipient does not have any allergies to certain plants.

Leaf and Flowers Tisanes / Good For:

BeeBalm (Bergamot)	fresh flower petals	Energy
Chamomile	dried and fresh flowers and leaves	Relaxation
Coriander	dried seeds	Indigestion
Dandelion	fresh young leaves	Fluid retention
Echinacea	dried or fresh flowers	Viruses
Elder - cooked berries *(NOT raw)*	also fresh flowers and leaves	Colds
Fennel	dried seeds	Indigestion
Ginger	fresh grated root	Nausea
Goldenseal	fresh flowers and leaves	Bladder
Hawthorn - berries *(NOT raw)*	also dried leaves and flowers	Heart-Circulation
Lavender	dried flowers	Relaxation
Lemon Balm	fresh leaves	Relaxation
Mint (all types)	dried and fresh leaves	IBS
Nettle	fresh young leaves	Tonic
Rose *(preferably damask)*	fresh buds	Relaxation
Rosemary	dried or fresh sprig	Headaches
Sage	dried or fresh leaves	Coughs
Vervain *(Verbena)*	dried or fresh leaves	Relaxation
Yarrow	fresh leaves and flowers	Digestion

Fruit Tisane:

A handful of dried berries gives a better flavour when hot water is poured over them.
Blackberry
Blueberry
Bilberry
Cranberry
Raspberry *(Do not use the leaves in tisanes, they can cause the womb to spasm)*
Strawberry

Similarly, dried pieces and rinds of other fruits give a stronger flavour in a tisane.
Apricot
Blackcurrant
Lemon
Lime
Orange
Passion Fruit
Peach
Red or White currants

Fruit cordials or squashes

A Cordial is a concentrated fruit or flower drink

made with sugar, that is diluted to make a pleasant drink. Cordials make wonderful gifts, if presented in nice bottles, so you need to start collecting some, or they can be bought quite cheaply online.

The main thing about a cordial is that the chosen fruit or flower has to have a strong taste to start with. Fruit has to be sharp, tart, acidic because you are going to add a lot of sugar to it. A bland, already sweet fruit, like pear, does not make a good cordial. A strongly scented flower like the elderflower makes a good cordial, with the addition of a little lemon juice. So does meadowsweet, some heavily scented roses, lavender and so on but we have decided to reserve flowers for our section on making Floral Syrups (see page 13).

How to make a cordial

Basically, it is a diluted form of jam or jelly making – fruit, some water and sugar. A fairly simple process.

1. Put washed fruit (minus any stalks, leaves etc) water (as per the table below) in a slow cooker or a heavy bottomed pan to simmer until the fruit is quite soft.
2. You now need to strain the fruit and juice through some muslin, without squeezing it in any way, in order to achieve a clear, impurity-free liquid.

    TIP: If you don't have jelly-making equipment (which is very cheap by the way) fill a new, clean pop sock, or a square of fine net curtaining, with the fruit and juice and suspend it over a large bowl. Whatever system you use, leave the pulp to drip overnight.

3. Put the juice back in a clean heavy bottomed pan. Ladle it out using a teacup and for every cup of juice add one cup of sugar.
4. Bring to the boil, turn down the heat and simmer for NO LONGER than five minutes.
5. Then pour the slightly-cooled cordial into warm, sterilised bottles.

    NOTE: Clean and sterilise bottles using sterilising tablets, dry and then lay them on a double tea towel in a baking tray and warm them on a very, very low oven. You want the bottles to be slightly warm when you pour the hot cordial into them.

Label your bottles, giving date made, ingredients, storage instructions (e.g. keep in fridge) and dilution instructions (e.g. one part cordial to three parts water or soda). Store in a cool, dry place until ready to gift. However, it is recommended that you make the cordials fairly close to the time that you intend to gift them.

RECIPES, INGREDIENTS AND PROPORTIONS
(We have suggested fruits here that do not require stones or pips removed)

Fruit	Other ingredients
Blackberry (2¼lb/1kg)	3 pints/1.8 litres water
Blackcurrant (2¼lb/1kg)	2 pints/1.2 litres water, 1 tablespoon tartaric acid
Elderberry (2¼/1kg)	2 pints/1.2 litres water
Lemon and Orange (zest and juice of 3 lemons & 3 oranges)	1 pint/600ml water, 1 tablespoon citric acid & 1 of tartaric acid
Lime (zest and juice of 6 limes)	1 pint/600ml water, 1 tablespoon citric acid & 1 of tartaric acid
Raspberry (2¼lb/1kg)	1¼ pints/625ml water, 6 tablespoons red wine vinegar

Bottled Fruit

Bottled fruit can be a very glamorous present to give family, friends or neighbours.

Especially useful if you have a glut of tree fruit, like plums.

Many people bottle fruit in Kilner jars but it is perfectly possible to use normal jam jars and buy lids and rubber rings from a specialist preserving company, quite cheaply. These rubber rings and lids are essential to get the absolutely airtight seal that is necessary to preserve the fruit until it is ready to be eaten.

Fruit can be bottled in syrup *or* water, but it should be noted that most experts recommend a sugar *and* water syrup because it keeps the flavour and colour of the fruit for longer. The best ratio of sugar to water is 8 ozs (225g) sugar to 1pt (600ml) water.

Of course, it is also possible to add liqueurs to the syrups to make the bottled fruit more exotic. Peaches, apricots, plums and cherries in brandy are popular but any liqueur could be added.

Note that bottled fruit has a measure of alcohol added to the syrup. This is not the same as a Rumtopf, where only alcohol is added to all the fruit in the pot, over a period, and you end up with a delicious mess of fruit, that has not retained its colour or shape.

With bottled fruit you are aiming for it to look good as well as taste nice. Therefore, it is important to choose fruit from your garden which is slightly underripe and firm. Do not use very ripe or overripe fruit, which will just turn into sludge in your jar. Save the very ripe fruit for making cordials or syrups for ice creams (See pages 4 and 13) Please mention on the jar label whether stones have been left in the fruit or not.

Cooking the fruit in their jars

For simplicity, we are suggesting what is called the 'oven method, wet pack'.

1. Pre-heat the oven to 150C/Gas 2/300F.
2. Line a large baking tray with several layers of newspaper. This prevents the jars from touching the hot metal of the baking tray and also soaks up any syrup in case it bubbles over.
3. Put the jars, open or without lids, on the baking tray – at least 2ins (5cms) space around each one and pop them in the oven for ten minutes to warm up.
4. Meanwhile, make the sugar syrup and put it in a pan over a moderate heat to simmer.
5. Remove the baking tray with the warm jars and fill the jars with the fruit, making sure that it is not too tightly packed in and comes just a little bit below the top rim of the jar.
6. Add the hot syrup solution to each jar, slowly, making sure you don't create bubbles and the syrup covers all the fruit in each jar.
7. Cover the jars with the rubber seals and lids but don't tighten.
8. Put in the oven for the recommended time (See overleaf).
9. Using heatproof gloves, remove the jars, one at a time and whilst still hot, firmly screw down or clip the jars closed. Wipe each jar down to remove any syrup that may have boiled over and put in a place to cool (NOT a sunny spot and NOT in the fridge or the jars may crack).
10. When cool, label the jars with the relevant information (e.g. Cherries in 50% sugar syrup) and date they were prepared.

NOTE: If bottling cherries, add 1 teaspoon of food grade citric acid powder to 4 pints (2 litres) of syrup solution.

Preparation of fruits and cooking times

Preparation	Cooking time

Apples *(preferably cookers)* — 30 – 40 minutes
Firm apples with no bruises and not too ripe.
Peel, core and cut into slices. *(Dip in lemon juice to stop browning)*

Apricots — 50 – 60 minutes
Wash, halve and stone.

Blackberries — 30 – 40 minutes
Must be firm, large and gently washed
to remove any bugs.

Blackcurrants/Redcurrants/Whitecurrants — 30 – 40 minutes
Firm but fully coloured. Wash, remove stalks
or any green currants gently.

Cherries — 40 – 50 minutes
Morello if possible, as they keep their
colour. Wash and remove stalks but not stones.

Damsons and Plums — 40 – 50 minutes
Choose firm but ripe fruit and they can be
bottled whole or cut in half and the stone removed.

Gooseberries — 40 – 50 minutes
Wash the berries and top and tail, taking a small slice
from the top and bottom of the berries as you do so.

Loganberries/Raspberries/Tayberries — 30 – 40 minutes
Choose firm but not green berries that retain their
shape when hulled. Leave in water for a little while
to allow excess seeds to detach themselves.

Preparation	Cooking time

Peaches
Need to skin them, which is easily done by pouring boiling water over them, then putting them in cold water and the skins rub off. Halve and stone.

50 – 60 minutes

Pears
Choose ripe but hard dessert pears with no blemishes. Peel and halve, cutting out the core.

60 – 70 minutes

Rhubarb
Wash sticks and cut up into even-sized pieces.

40 – 50 minutes

NOTE: If a fruit is not listed (e.g. strawberries) it is because it does not bottle well, often losing flavour, shape and colour.

Jam

The great thing about jam is that it is actually very easy to make as long as you are not entering some competition that demands aesthetically perfect preserves. Most people will be very happy to receive a gift of ordinary jam, without pips, skin or whole fruit in – and this is the method we are going to present to you here. The old fashioned method that does not require any fancy thermometers or equipment.

1. First, sterilise your jam jars and lids. The simplest method of doing this is to fill a large clean bowl with water, put in your clean empty jars and pop in a sterilising tablet (the type used to sterilise babies bottles) and leave them until you have finished the jam making process.

2. Next, if you have a slow cooker, then put your clean fruit in it (no water), turn it on to low and leave it on for at least four hours. This will draw out the maximum amount of pectin in the fruit. (See the table overleaf). High pectin fruit needs to be mixed with something low pectin or it will come out as a solid mass that you can cut with a knife! If you don't have a slow cooker, then put your fruit in a covered casserole dish and put it in a low oven. *Note: Dried fruit needs soaking in water overnight before cooking slowly.*

3. Once the fruit has cooked slowly, push it all through a standard sieve into a large measuring jug. You should end up with juice and fruit pulp. Now, the rule is to add 1lb (450g) of sugar to each pint (600ml) of juice and pulp.

4. Make sure the sugar is thoroughly dissolved in the fruit mixture and put it on a medium heat, so that you will get what is called a 'rolling boil' (that's a bit more than a simmer). What you want for this is a long handled wooden spoon, so that you can give the occasional stir to make sure it's not sticking and, hopefully, not get burnt by spitting hot jam!

5. Whilst the jam is bubbling, put a china saucer in the freezer for a little while. After about ten minutes, take the ice cold saucer out and drop a little of the bubbling jam on to it. Wait for a minute and then push the cooled drop of jam with your finger. If it wrinkles and stays where you have pushed it, the jam is ready. If it doesn't, wipe the saucer with some kitchen paper and put it back in the freezer. This procedure may have to be repeated every five minutes or so, depending upon the fruit you are using. Some jams set quicker than others.

6. Turn off the jam and cover, meanwhile remove your sterilised jam jars and wipe them dry with kitchen paper. Stand them all on a double layer of kitchen paper and gradually fill them with the cooled jam, up to the bottom of the jar neck. Put a double layer of kitchen paper over the tops of the filled, open jars and allow them to give off steam as they cool. This will make the kitchen paper a little damp.

7. Once the jam is completely cold, pop a waxed circle over the jam itself (available online from many sources) and screw the lids on. You may choose to cover the lids with fabric or pretty paper and make attractive labels for the jars.

The pectin levels of fruit

The higher the pectin level of a fruit, the firmer the jam will set. So it is advisable to mix fruits – high with low – like apple and late blackberry – to get a medium consistency to a jam.

It is also possible to add substances to medium/low pectin fruit when making jam, such as special jam sugar which has added pectin (available in most large supermarkets). Adding lemon juice to low pectin fruits can often help. Do not, however, use the pectin-enriched sugar or lemon juice if you are making a jam from high pectin fruit, or it will become very solid!

HIGH	MEDIUM	LOW
Apples *(Cooking)*	Apples *(eating)*	Apricots *(fresh)*
Apples *(Crab)*	Apricots *(dried)*	Blackberries *(late)*
Blackcurrants	Blackberries *(early)*	Blueberries
Chilean Guavas *(also known as Strawberry Myrtle)*	Cherries *(sour)*	Cherries *(sweet)*
Cranberries *(fresh and dried)*	Elderberries	Figs
Damsons	Greengages	Guavas
Gooseberries	Loganberries	Mulberries
Grapes	Raspberries	Melon
Plums		Nectarines
Quinces		Pears
Redcurrants		Peaches
White currants		Pomegranates
		Rhubarb
		Strawberries

Floral Syrups

You only need small amounts of these gorgeous perfumed and delicately coloured syrups. They are used to drizzle over desserts, like ice cream or meringues, or can be used in cocktails.

Very, very simple to make.

1. Put 1 pint (600ml) water in a heavy bottomed saucepan. Add 1lb (450g) sugar (ordinary caster sugar).

2. Bring to the boil and then turn heat down to a simmer until the mixture reduces, thickens and coats the back of a wooden spoon. (Make sure it doesn't burn round the sides of the pan by giving it frequent stirrings).

3. Turn off the heat, add the washed flower heads, petals or buds, press down a little, then cover the pan and leave to infuse for a day.

4. Remove the flowers and strain the syrup, before putting in small bottles and labelling.

TIP : You can add a tiny amount of food colouring to the cold syrup if you feel that it would enhance the look.

Suggested Flowers and Quantities

Elderflowers: about 15 heads of flowers

Lavender: 8 tablespoons of lavender flowers *(removed from central stem)*

Lilacs: 5 or 6 handfuls of flowers

Meadowsweet: 10 modest handfuls of flowers

Roses: 4 modest handfuls of petals *(preferably dark red scented variety)*

Dried fruits

If you have a huge amount of fruit in your garden, then it is worth investing in a proper dehydrating cabinet. However, if, like most of us, you have gluts of fruit, where you want to make the most of the produce whilst it is available, then drying fruits in the oven for consumption later, is really easy.

The size of the fruit for drying is your choice, depending upon how you want to use it. If, for example, you want to gift dried fruit to be used as part of breakfast cereal or added to yoghurt, then you might want to chop larger fruit, like apples, pears, apricots and plums into small bite-size chunks. Berries and currants, of course, can be left whole. Strawberries are usually cut into slices.

For gifting as dried fruit snacks, people often like to receive fruit in larger portions. Apples and pears can be cut into ring or slices, apricots and plums should be halved, and the stones removed. If you are lucky enough to have nectarines or peaches in your garden or greenhouse, then they also can be sliced after the removal of the stones. Apples and pears, once cut, should be put in a bowl of cold water and lemon juice, until they go into the oven, to prevent discolouration.

Whatever you choose, make sure that each batch of fruit going into the oven is roughly the same size, so that they dry at the same rate.

HOW TO DRY FRUITS IN THE OVEN

1. Wash and dry your chosen fruit/s, remove any stones and cut to the required size.

2. Spread the fruit out in a single layer on a baking tray lined with a double layer of greaseproof paper (this is to stop the metal baking tray burning the skin of the smaller fruits. If you are drying halves of fruit – like apricots or plums, put the cut side upwards.

3. Starting with a very, very low oven – 50C/120F/Gas Mark 0 – it is then a waiting game. With small chunks it should take about 2 hours at this temperature and then, perhaps another 2 at 65C/150F/Gas Mark ½. You want the fruit to be chewy not crisp, but you want it to be dried out thoroughly so that it stores well. With larger fruit halves it could take 3 hours to get to the stage where the skins begin to shrivel and you then raise the temperature, as previously advised, for another 3 hours.

4. When dried, the fruit needs to be removed and allowed to cool naturally (covered with a tea towel) for a good 8 hours.

5. Then pack into airtight glass jars or cellophane bags (not plastic, it makes things sweat), Label with the types of fruit and date they should be eaten by. (6 months from the date they were dried should be safe, providing they are stored well).

Fruit leathers

These are wonderful snacks and absolutely adored by children! Very easy to make *(see next page)*. You can mix fruits to make interesting and tangy flavours. One of the best flavours is what I call Summer Fruit. It's when you just use handfuls of every berry harvested on that day from the garden. So, frequently, it is a mixture of blueberries, blackberries, blackcurrants, strawberries, redcurrants and raspberries! If you don't grow fruits in any great volume, you can easily freeze berries each day, and use them to make the leathers when you have stored enough to make it worthwhile.

FRUIT LEATHERS – HOW TO MAKE THEM

1. Wash and dry 1½lbs (675g) berries (you could add stoned cherries as well).
2. Add to a heavy bottomed pan with 4 tablespoons runny honey, 2 tablespoons lemon juice and 2 tablespoons of water.
3. Cook on a low heat (or better still cook on low in a slow cooker) until the fruit breaks down and becomes mushy.
4. Let the fruit mush cool down and then either mash it even more by hand, spritz it with a hand blender or put in a food processor until you have a smooth puree.
5. Heat your oven to 140C/275F/Gas Mark 1.
6. Line a baking tray with greaseproof paper or a silicone baking sheet.
7. Spread the fruit puree out in the baking tray, trying to get the thickness uniform (you shouldn't be able to see the greaseproof paper underneath).
8. Put the tray of puree in the oven for at least 6 hours, turning the tray occasionally – especially if your oven tends to get warmer at the back.
9. Test whether it is ready by fingertip. It should be slightly tacky but not hard. With a palette knife try and lift a corner of the puree. It is done if it raises in a single piece.
10. Remove and whilst warm, cut into strips, or you can roll into tubes, as in the picture.
11. When cold pack into cellophane bags and label.

Infused *vinegars*

You can infuse white wine, rice, white currant, sherry or light cider vinegar with almost any plant flavour – herbs, fruits, or flowers. Never use malt or balsamic vinegar though. Their flavours are too strong and pungent to be infused. Infused vinegars are wonderful in salad dressings or as a base for creating an Oriental sauce. Vinegars that are infused with berries (like raspberry or blackberry) are usually sweetened with honey or sugar and diluted, like a cordial, or taken neat, by the spoonful, as an astringent digestive tonic.

How to make herb vinegars

Very simple. In a large jam jar *(or two – with vinegar proof lids – these are lined with plastic)* fill a third of it with the crushed *(to release the oils)* herbs of your choice. Tarragon, dill, thyme, garlic, chives are all good flavours but really you can choose any herbs you wish and add lemon or lime slices as well. Then top the jar up with the vinegar of your choice. Seal the jar and put it on a windowsill or in a greenhouse where it will get the sun for about two weeks. Then strain it through a fine sieve or muslin into a fresh bottle or jam jar. Add a sprig or two of fresh herbs into the bottle for decoration and label.

RECIPE FOR FRUIT VINEGAR

1lb (450g) washed fruit *(berries work best)*
1lb (450g) caster sugar
1 pint (600ml) white vinegar of your choice

Put the fruit in a glass, china or Pyrex bowl *(not metal, silicon or plastic)*. Crush the fruit a little to release the juices.

Add the vinegar and cover the top of the bowl with a china dinner plate and leave for one week to infuse.

Strain the liquid through a fine sieve into an enamel or steel saucepan.

Put it on a low heat while you stir in the sugar until it is dissolved.

Boil for ten minutes, allow to cool and then bottle and label.

Infused oils

Cooking oils that are infused with herbs are incredibly useful and look very dramatic.

The finished oils can be used for salad dressings or for rubbing into meat or fish prior to roasting.

It is important to use dried herbs, as fresh herbs contain moisture, which can produce moulds or can cause the oil to become rancid. Dried herbs have stronger flavours than fresh herbs, however, so use less.

There are two suggested ways of creating a herbal oil for culinary use (see opposite). Given that you will possibly be making Christmas gifts with the dried herbs and sunlight, in the autumn/winter, could be intermittent, we suggest that you use the quick method. However, if you are making a gift of infused oil for someone in the summer, then you could use the slow, sunlight-dependent method.

You can use one herb, like rosemary, to infuse an oil, or a mixture of savoury herbs. Or you can infuse oil for a specific purpose for, say, rubbing into fish, so combining dried lemon slices and zest with herbs.

Always label the gifted bottle with a full description of what oil and herbs have been combined; how to use the oil; how to store it and for how long.

The slow method of infusing oil

1. Put several tablespoons of your chosen dried herbs in a large sterilised jar.
2. Fill to the top with your chosen oil.
3. Screw on the lid tightly and shake to distribute the herbs.
4. Place the jar on a sunny windowsill.
5. Shake the jar once a day.
6. After two weeks, strain the mixture through a fine sieve or muslin cloth. (You may have to do this a couple of times – washing the sieve in between or using a fresh muslin cloth.)
7. Put the strained oil into a sterilised bottle.
8. Label the bottle clearly (see opposite).
9. If you wish, place some dried whole sprigs, of herbs, into the bottle as decoration.

The quick method of infusing oil

1. It is necessary to have a slow method of heating the oil and herbs. A slow cooker or an electric yoghurt maker would be ideal. Otherwise gently warm the oil and herbs in a pan and put the mixture into a large thermos flask and seal.
2. If you use any of the above methods, leave the mixture to infuse for 24 hours (as long as your slow cooker actually does produce a very low heat – some don't).
3. Turn off the heat, or open the thermos, and allow the infused oil mixture to cool.
4. Follow steps 6 to 9 of the Slow Method.

Suggested oils and flavourings to use

Oils
Virgin olive oil
Sunflower oil
Sesame oil
Groundnut oil
Walnut oil.

NOTE: Infused oil will last for six months but it should be stored in a cool, dark place.

Herbs and other flavourings
Basil
Bouquet Garni *(bay, thyme and parsley)*
Chervil
Chili peppers *(but be sparing, dried chilis are powerful!)*
Coriander seeds *(crushed)*
Garlic *(dried or fresh if using the quick method of infusion)*
Lemon balm
Lemon grass
Lemon rind
Lemon verbena
Marjoram
Oregano
Rosemary
Thyme

NOTE: Experiment with combinations! See what works for you and what you think others may like.

Dried herb Parcels or Pots

These can be bundles of dried herbs in a muslin sachet or parcel (like the picture), which are meant to be added to soups and stew as a complete parcel and fished out before the dish is served. Or, herbs are dried and processed (either with a pestle and mortar or food processor) and kept in jars or packets to be sprinkled over, or added to, a dish before cooking. Put several herb bags in a tin or cardboard box and label it prettily, or gift loose herbs in jars with cotton covers on the lids and atractive labels.

Once herbs are dried, they should be kept out of bright light, away from the damp, and used within six months.

Bouquet Garni

Flavouring for stocks, stews and soups. Anything that needs long slow cooking. The herbs should preferably kept in their whole state (not ground), put in a muslin bag, sachet or pouch and tied up with long ties, so that it can be easily lifted out when cooking has finished.

BASIC COMBINATION

a bay leaf, a sprig of thyme, 3 sprigs of any type of parsley.

EXTRA COMBINATION

a bay leaf, a sprig of thyme, 3 sprigs of any kind of parsley, a teaspoon of dried celery seeds, dried garlic or dried fennel.

Fines Herbes

This combination of herbs is particularly good sprinkled on omelettes or quiches before cooking.
The herbs should be dried and ground, then stored in bags or jars so that a generous spoonful can removed easily when required.

BASIC MIXTURE

chervil, tarragon, parsley and chives in equal measure.

EXTRA MIXTURE

as above but with the addition of basil, oregano and sage.

Italian Herb Mixture

A good mixture for sprinkling on pizzas, pasta and into sauces. Should be gifted in pots or jars.

BASIC MIXTURE

50% oregano with the addition of 10% of each of the following: rosemary, tarragon, basil, thyme and sage. Grind all together, mix thoroughly and pot up.

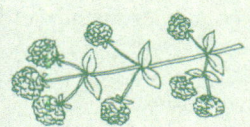

Herbes de Provence

A more aromatic French mixture, which is often sold in Provence in pretty cotton bags. However, putting it in a jar will keep the herbs dry and make the aromas last longer. Traditionally, the mixture is sprinkled over grilled foods, like chicken and fish.

BASIC MIXTURE

equal measures of dried thyme, basil, rosemary, tarragon, savory, marjoram, oregano, and a few bay leaves.

Dried Peas and Beans

Not all beans and peas are suitable for drying. Runner beans, mangetout and similar, where you eat the whole pod, are better used fresh or frozen. But there are many beans and peas that you can successfully dry and keep and they make welcome gifts for anyone's store cupboard (see opposite).

Once your beans and peas are dried and cooled they can be stored in, ideally, airtight glass jars – Kilner or other glass storage jars – or in cellophane bags. Do not store them in plastic bags because they will sweat. Jars of dried beans are best stored in a cool dark place.

If gifting beans and peas, then you must label them carefully with the type of bean or pea, the date they were dried and the instructions for preparation for use. Because beans have a large amount of a substance called lectin, which can cause stomach problems, it is necessary for them to be soaked overnight to rehydrate them. Then to be boiled in fresh water for at least ten minutes and simmered until soft.

There are several methods of drying beans and peas, which are described opposite.

Methods of drying

In the pod

Traditionally, the method was to let the pods hang on the plant for as long as possible, then uproot the plant and hang it somewhere warm and dry. This allowed the pods to become so dry that, if you shook them, you could hear the beans/peas rattle inside the dried pod. But you can only rely on this method if you have a guaranteed warm and dry climate. The slightest suspicion of damp can cause the beans and peas to grow mould.

If you use either of the following two drying methods, the beans/peas need to be podded into cold salt water first (to kill off any little maggots or insects). Then they should be blanched in boiling water for a couple of minutes before drying them off with paper towels before they are air-dried.

A dehydrator

This is basically an electric table-top air-drying machine, that allows for the gentle drying of layers of garden produce. They are simple to use, come with a full set of instructions and are quite reasonably priced. But investing in one is probably only something you would do if you intended to dry a substantial amount of fruit and veg.

In the oven

To dry beans and peas you need to be able to run an oven on a very low heat. Electric fan ovens are considered to be the best for this job and gas ovens, unfortunately, not so good.

Spread the beans/peas out in a thin layer on greaseproof paper in a large baking tray. Set the oven at 50C/120F for one hour, then increase the temperature to 70C/150F for another two hours. At the end of this drying period the beans/peas should be quite hard. Allow to cool and then pack in jars and label.

Types of beans or peas that can be successfully dried

Adzuki *(probably best grown in a greenhouse)*	Haricot or Navy bean *(may need to be grown in a greenhouse in some areas)*
Broad beans	Kidney
Borlotti	Lentil
Cannellini *(type of haricot bean)*	Marrowfat peas
Chickpeas *(probably best grown in a greenhouse)*	Petit pois
	Pinto
Edamame *(type of soybean)*	Split pea
Flageolet *(small underripe haricot beans)*	

Nuts

If you are lucky enough to have a nut tree in your garden, then you will be very popular if you can gift roasted chestnuts, hazelnuts or cobnuts, when in season. These three nuts are the most likely to be grown in gardens in the northern hemisphere. Exotic nuts like almond, pine, pistachio, pecan, cashew, macadamia and walnut are usually found in warmer climates – although it's possible that they are grown by some intrepid souls in large heated greenhouses and conservatories! Peanuts, of course, are not tree nuts. They are legumes, grown underground.

We are going to suggest that you roast your garden nuts and then store them in a cool, dark place in glass containers, until you are ready to gift them. Then you can toss them into one of the flavourings we recommend here and re-toast them briefly to seal in the flavours.

Seeds

These are easier to grow in the average garden – pumpkin (or any winter squash), flax and sunflower being the easiest. Please remember that, at the time of writing, growing hemp without a license is illegal, but flax seeds are similar, if a little smaller. Sesame plants can be grown for seeds too, but they require constant warmth, so possibly need to be grown in a greenhouse or on a sunny windowsill indoors.

How to prepare and roast seeds

1. Once you have collected your seeds, you should wash them. This is a challenge with pumpkin seeds, as you will need to separate them from the clingy pulp of the pumpkin. It is suggested that you boil the seeds in salty water for about ten minutes and the pulp will easily come away from the seeds.

2. All seeds should be thoroughly dried after washing, then you need to place them in a bowl with the mix of seasonings that you are using (see below). Make sure the seeds are thoroughly coated before laying them out in a single layer on a baking tray lined with greaseproof paper.

3. Roast in a moderate oven (160C/325F/Gas Mark3) for about twenty minutes. But keep a careful eye on them. You don't want them to burn.

SESAME SEEDS, being very small and oily, need only about eight minutes of roasting, so process them separately from larger seeds.

NUTS also only require roasting for a maximum of ten minutes and, if you are doing several types of nuts together, then chop them, so that they are all the same size and will all cook evenly.

Recipes for flavourings for roasted nuts and seeds

SWEET

(For a batch of 4ozs (100g) nuts or seeds)

1 oz (25g) melted butter

1 oz (25g) melted coconut oil

3 tablespoons of honey

1 teaspoon of cinnamon

½ teaspoon ground nutmeg

SAVOURY

(For a batch of 4ozs (100g) of nuts or seeds)

1oz (25g) melted butter

½ teaspoon garlic salt

½ teaspoon black pepper

½ teaspoon powdered chili pepper (optional)

1 teaspoon of Worcestershire sauce

ROASTING CHESTNUTS

Heat the oven to 180C/350F/Gas Mark 4. Put chestnuts into hot, still water for one hour. Drain and pat dry. Cut a cross in the base of each chestnut and put them on a baking tray. Roast for 30 minutes until the outer shell begins to come away. Serve warm.

Pickles

Pickling is really very simple and if you don't like the smell of simmering vinegar (see Chutneys on page 28), then you can stick to making crisp pickles, which require you to only use cold, spiced vinegar.

Vegetables for pickling need to be young and firm, otherwise they won't keep, once pickled. Baby beetroots are ideal, or, if larger, then sliced or diced into smaller pieces. Small onions, cucumbers, gherkins etc. are preferred.

You can buy special pickling vinegar, which contains spices, or you can make your own. A white vinegar is preferred (so that you can see the colour of the vegetables). A malt vinegar is best, but you can, if you wish, use white wine vinegar, but it must have an acidity level of at least 5 percent.

You will need to pack your pickles into jars with vinegar-proof lids. These are lids with a plastic inner lining. Anything else will corrode. Get your friends to save jars from their shop-bought pickles (except from piccalilli which tends to turn the inside of the lids yellow).

Recipe for spiced vinegar

2 pints (1.2 litre) vinegar

Now add the following spices together, tied in a muslin bag:

½ tspn (7g) cinnamon (preferably bark not powdered)

½ tspn (7g) whole cloves

½ tspn (7g) peppercorns (any colour)

½ tspn (7g) mace

½ tspn (7g) allspice berries

1 oz (25g) mustard seeds

2 bay leaves

Put the vinegar in an enamel or stainless steel heavy bottomed pan, with a lid. Bring it to the boil for no more than a minute. Turn off the heat, add the muslin bag with the spices. Put the lid on and also cover the lid with a folded up tea towel. Leave the spices to steep in the vinegar for a few hours, then remove the spices and bottle the vinegar. *(Label it to make sure you don't use it for something other than pickles!)*

PICKLED ONION/SHALLOTS

Make some brine. This involves dissolving, by gentle simmering, 1lb (450g) of salt in 2½ pints (1.5 litres) of water. When the salt has dissolved and the brine is quite cold, put your unpeeled onions or shallots into half of the brine (weight them down in their brine bath with a saucepan lid) and leave them all day. Then drain them, peel and put them in the other half of the brine and leave them for 24 hours. Then rinse them very well, put them into suitable jars and cover with the cold spiced pickling vinegar.

Label the jar but don't gift them for a couple of months because they need to mature and develop full flavour.

PICKLED BEETROOT

Choose whole baby beetroot. Wash carefully (Don't break the skin). Boil for approx. 2 hours (A slow cooker on high is best). Skin, pack into jars and cover with cold spiced vinegar.

PICKLED CAULIFLOWER

The same method as for pickled onions, except cut them into similar size pieces and only give them one brine bath of 24 hours. Drain, rinse, pack into jars and cover with the spiced vinegar.

PICKLED RED CABBAGE and PICKLED CUCUMBER/GHERKIN

Both of these vegetables need to be washed and sliced and layered with salt. So put one layer in a large dish, cover with a very generous layer of salt. Do another layer in the same manner. Leave for 24 hours. Rinse well. Pat dry with kitchen paper and pack into jars. Cover with the cold, spiced vinegar.

A PICKLED MIXTURE

Onions, cauliflower and cucumber/gherkin combine well in a jar, but beetroot and red cabbage are best left in their own jars. The onion and cauliflower have to be prepared differently, of course, before combining everything and adding the vinegar.

Chutneys

Unlike pickling, where the fruit needs to be hard and young, chutneys can use up older fruit and vegetables, providing they are not overripe or bruised. They are also great for using up small amounts of fruit and vegetables, as everything is diced into small sizes. Chutneys, of course, are wonderful served with curries, cheese or cold meats.

RECIPE AND METHOD FOR A BASIC APPLE CHUTNEY

Makes about 4lbs (1.8 kg) – should fill up to 6 jars, depending on their size. Don't forget you need jars with vinegar proof lids.

1 pint (600ml) spiced white pickling vinegar (see page 27)
2 lb (900g) apples, peeled, cored and chopped
1 lb (450g) white sugar
12ozs (325g) sultanas or golden raisins
1½ teaspoons table salt
1oz (25g) ground ginger
1oz (25g) mustard seed
½ teaspoon pepper (*any pepper – black, white, cayenne*)
1 teaspoon ground allspice

1. Put all ingredients, except the apples and sultanas, into a big enamel or steel saucepan and bring to the boil. Stir carefully to make sure the sugar has completely dissolved.
2. Add apples and turn the heat down to simmer the mixture for ten minutes. Add the sultanas.
3. Simmer, occasionally stirring, until the mixture thickens.
4. The chutney is done when you can draw a spoon through the mixture and leave a definite indent that slowly fills back up again.
5. Allow the chutney to cool slightly before pouring into sterilised jars and covering the open jars with kitchen paper until completely cold.
6. Put on the lids, label with ingredients and store in a cool, dry place until ready to gift.

The *ultimate sauce* from the *garden*

Peperonata is an amazingly versatile sauce – which can be used as a base for pizzas, as a chunky dip, on toast as bruschetta or a sauce for pasta. The great thing about it is that it uses up so many vegetables and herbs that you probably have growing in your garden. It keeps, unopened, for a long time, although it is best to keep your jars in the back of the fridge, if you have room. Trust me, once you have gifted peperonata, people will keep coming back for more of this versatile and delicious sauce.

INGREDIENTS

2 tablespoons olive oil

1 large onion

2 or 3 cloves of garlic (or 1 dessertspoon of garlic paste)

1 tablespoon chopped dried herbs such as parsley, oregano, celery leaf, rosemary etc. If you use fresh herbs, it would be best to put them in a muslin bag. Add it when adding the tomatoes and remove when filling up the jars.

Salt and pepper to taste

8 to 10 peppers – mix of sweet and hot, depending upon taste

2lb (900g) of skinned and chopped ripe tomatoes

1 tspn chipotle chili paste

1 tspn smoked paprika paste

METHOD

Deseed peppers and cut into strips. Chop onion finely. Heat oil in pan and saute onion for 5 minutes.

Add peppers and crushed garlic and cook for a few more minutes.

Add tomatoes and herbs, cover and simmer until peppers are very soft.

Remove lid, raise the heat and cook until excess liquid has evaporated.

Add salt and pepper to taste.

Fill sterilised jars and label. Keep in fridge until giving them as presents and advise the recipient to keep it in the fridge before and during use.

Savoury Dip

Nothing will make you more popular than if you conjure up some tasty dips for neighbourhood parties or family get-togethers, using fresh ingredients from your garden. And the great thing is that you can create some completely different dips, in taste and appearance, with one basic recipe.

THE BASE RECIPE FOR ONE DIP

7ozs (200g) plain cream cheese
4ozs (100g) plain yoghurt
Small pinch of salt
A sprinkling of pepper
(Please note that you could use vegan cream 'cheese' and plain soya yoghurt as an alternative)

Suggested flavourings for different dips

(Add to the basic mixture above and mix well)

Spicy Beetroot
4 pureed/mashed cooked baby beetroot
2 cloves minced garlic
½ teaspoon each of ground cumin paprika and chopped fresh coriander.

Roasted Carrot
4 medium sized carrots, cut into chunks and roasted in a little oil in a hot oven for about 25 minutes. Mash and add 2 cloves minced garlic and half teaspoon of cayenne pepper.

Cheese and Chive
4ozs (100g) grated hard cheese
(could be a vegan alternative)
a bunch of finely chopped chives
2 cloves of minced garlic and additional pepper to taste.

Hot Courgette
3 medium courgettes, cut into thick slices and briefly grilled on both sides
1 deseeded, halved and grilled chili pepper
1 clove garlic
1 tablespoon of tahini.
Puree everything together.

Make your own mustard

Amazingly, mustard plants are part of the cabbage family! After flowering, the plants produce seed pods. These should be left to dry, in a paper bag, until they are a tan/brown colour and very papery. If you then break them open, they will be full of seeds. Mustard seeds are usually, white, black or brown and here we have recipes for the most popular types of mustards, which are easy to make and store. We have given small quantity recipes here. Mustards should be stored in a glass jar and left for at least one week for the favour to develop. Experiment with the recipes to achieve the taste, quantity and thickness you prefer.

American Mustard

2 tablespoons powdered white mustard seeds
1 tablespoon white wine
1 tablespoon vinegar
1 teaspoon sugar
Mix together until smooth.

Bordeaux Mustard

1 tablespoons of crushed black or brown mustard seeds
1 tablespoon powdered white mustard seeds
2 tablespoons red wine
2 cloves of crushed garlic
1 tablespoon of very finely chopped tarragon and marjoram
2 teaspoons of sugar.

Dijon Mustard

2 tablespoons powdered white or brown mustard seeds
2 tablespoons white wine
1 crushed garlic clove
1 tablespoon runny honey
1 tablespoon olive oil
Large pinch of salt.

English Mustard

2 tablespoons powdered white mustard seeds
½ teaspoon cayenne pepper
½ teaspoon turmeric powder
large pinch of salt
½ teaspoon runny honey
4 tablespoons of half water/half vinegar.

Flavoured butters and cheeses

Flavoured butters with herbs, fruit or flowers (like orange, lemon or lime zest or lavender), are a fantastic addition to your store cupboard and, if presented nicely, can be a wonderful gift, or your contribution to a neighbourhood or family party. You can freeze butters too, which is useful. Butters look charming when they are moulded into a roll, so that they can be cut into slices to go straight on to fish, meat, poultry or bread.

Soft cheeses (cream, cottage, goat) do not freeze well, so it is best to prepare them when you intend to gift them. Once you have mixed the flavours into a cheese, then put it into a nice pot, which can be placed in the centre of a party table, surrounded by bread or crackers.

Always label the finished butters or cheeses with ingredients and suggested use.

RECIPES

Mash the following finely chopped ingredients into 4ozs (100g) creamed butter or soft cheese:

1. 3 tablespoons fresh parsley, 1 garlic clove, 1 tablespoon lemon juice, 1 teaspoon fresh ground black pepper. *(This flavoured butter is great for cooking fish)*
2. 1 garlic clove, half a tablespoon each of tarragon, chervil, chives and parsley. *(The butter is perfect for making garlic bread. The cheese is for spreading on bread)*
3. 1 garlic clove, 1 tablespoon of dried, ground chili peppers, 1 tablespoon chives. *(Either butter or cheese can be used to melt into cooked steaks or pork shanks. The cheese is a marvellous party spread.)*

SECTION 2: *Health & Beauty*

Fruit Tonics

These take the form of syrups, but they are not to be confused with cough syrups, which we feature on page 6. A dessertspoonful of these syrups can be taken daily, as a valuable source of vitamins and antioxidants.

ELDERBERRY ROB

An ancient remedy supposed to ward off colds and also ease them if they do take hold.

1lb (450g) elderberries

½pt (300ml) water

½lb (225g) light brown sugar

4 cloves

2 cinnamon sticks

¼pt (150ml) orange juice

1. Remove all berries from their stalks. Put the berries and water into a slow cooker, if possible, and cook on low for 2 hours. Halfway through the cooking period, mash the elderberries a little with a potato masher, to extract more juice.

2. Allow the slow cooker to cool, then strain the liquid through a metal sieve into a bowl. (Not a nylon sieve, as you will never get the elderberry stains out) Leave the sieve to drip into the bowl for an hour.

3. Put all the juice into a stainless steel pan (not enamel, as it will stain) add the sugar and stir to dissolve (using a metal or black silicon spoon – again because of staining).
4. Add the cloves, cinnamon and orange juice and let the mixture simmer (a lively simmer but not a boil) for about half an hour or when it becomes syrupy and coats the back of the spoon.
5. Remove the spices with a slotted spoon. Allow the mixture to cool, then bottle and label.

NOTE: This syrup can be taken either as a dessertspoonful a day to help ward off colds (as it is packed with vitamin C), or you can put a small amount in a cup and dilute with the same amount of hot water to drink when you feel you actually have a cold. Elderberries can be replaced with blackberries or blackcurrants, if preferred.

ROSEHIP AND APPLE SYRUP

Packed with Vitamin C and antioxidants.
NOTE: The rosehips need to be ripe, which means they are not rock hard.

1lb (450g) washed rosehips (top and tail like gooseberries).
1lb (450g) apples, peeled cored and cubed (any type of apple)
1lb (450g) sugar (white granulated)
4 pints (2.4 litres) water

1. Mash up rosehips and apples in a food processor.
2. Use a large stainless steel or enamel pan. Put the water and fruit in the pan and boil for about ten minutes.
3. Strain the water and pulp through a sieve into a bowl. Allow the sieve to drip into the bowl for about an hour, then gently press the pulp (but not through the sieve, just to extract the last amount of juice.
4. Return the fruit-flavoured water to a clean pan, add the sugar and stir with a long-handled wooden spoon until the sugar is dissolved.
5. Simmer the contents of the pan (without any lid) until the contents have reduced a little and become syrupy (when it coats the back of a wooden spoon). Don't over-boil it or it will turn into a substance more like jam.
6. When cooled, bottle and label. Keep in the fridge until gifted.

Footbaths

Folk medicine has always maintained that having a hot bath at the onset of a virus will help to shorten its duration and severity. It could be because a hot bath stimulates the circulation and lymph glands, encouraging them to remove toxins; it also makes you perspire a little – again another way for the body to expel toxins – and usually stimulates the production of urine, yet another way of eliminating a virus.

However, before the invention of modern plumbing, filling up an entire bath with hot water was a huge effort – so the footbath was invented. Ancient Chinese medicine holds that points on the feet are linked to various parts of the body. Modern reflexologists base their foot treatments on these ancient principles, and foot massage is usually preceded by a herbal footbath.

In short, a footbath infused with various plants is a good idea. Not only is it a treat for the feet but you are inhaling the infusions and treating your body and mind as well. A hot (but not scalding) footbath can help to alleviate tired and aching feet and help other problems as well.

NOTE: Do not use any footbath if you have any broken skin on your feet. Wait for cuts, grazes or blisters to heal before attempting a footbath.

OLD FASHIONED MUSTARD BATH

This bath is supposed to improve circulation, ease aching and be good for arthritis.

2 dessert spoons of crushed mustard seeds

2 sprigs of bruised rosemary

3 dried meadowsweet flower clusters, crumbled into the footbath

ACHING FEET BATH

This is for feet that are not arthritic but are just aching from standing or walking.

3 dried meadowsweet flower clusters, crumbled into the footbath

3 tablespoons of dried, crumbled St. John's Wort flowers

¼pt (150ml) white wine vinegar in which a handful of sage leaves have been simmered for about five minutes (add the vinegar and leaves to the footbath).

AN ANTI-FUNGAL FOOTBATH

All of the plants recommended here are anti-fungal and antiseptic. Obviously, if you have a very bad case of fungus you need to see a doctor. If it is just mild, it is worth trying this footbath twice a week, at least, for a couple of weeks, to see if there is an improvement.

You can try a handful of each of these herbs in your footbath, in combination, or select just one:

Thyme (fresh leaves, bruised)

Basil (fresh leaves, bruised)

Lemongrass (fresh, chopped up or minced, like garlic)

Mint (fresh leaves, bruised)

Garlic (two cloves, minced) (You may choose to stick to the nice-smelling herbs!)

SLEEP-AID FOOTBATH

Inhale a few lungfuls of the gentle steam and perfumes of the footbath before you put it on the floor and put your feet in it.

Lavender (two small handfuls of dried flowers)

Hops (two small handfuls crumbled dried hops)

1 teaspoon of dried and powdered valerian root

(Sweet dreams!)

Cough Syrups

Gentle syrups made with the addition of plants, as part of the infusion, have actually worked well for centuries to alleviate coughs. Obviously, if your chest becomes so congested that you have trouble breathing, then you should seek medical advice as you may have a chest infection, which requires medical intervention. But, as an aid to relieving the congestion of a cold, homemade syrups can work very well. (See also Fruit Tonics on page 24)

BASIC PLANT SYRUP

1. Take 3 handfuls of your chosen plant (see the list opposite. Only use one type of plant, do not mix)
2. Put plant parts in a stainless steel or enamel pan and put in just enough water to cover.
3. Heat the mixture until simmering, then turn off the heat, cover with a tight-fitting lid and leave the mixture to infuse for 24 hours.
4. Pour the mixture through a sieve into a measuring jug or bowl. Discard the plants.
5. For each teacup of liquid that you ladle into a clean saucepan, add one teacup full of white sugar.
6. Stir to dissolve the sugar and heat the mixture to achieve a consistent simmer. Continue to stir to make sure that the sugar isn't sticking to the bottom of the pan.
7. The syrup is ready when it coats the back of a wooden spoon.
8. Allow to cool and pour into sterilised bottles and label.
9. Take two teaspoons twice a day.

GRANDMA'S ONION SYRUP

2 large strong flavoured onions • Honey (if you can get real Manuka Honey, that just adds to the benefit) OR unrefined brown sugar

1. Peel and slice the onions *(onion tears are also a good way to decongest the sinuses, by the way).*
2. Put a layer of onion slices in a bowl *(preferably glass or pyrex)*
3. Drizzle over with honey or sprinkle one dessertspoon of brown sugar.
4. Repeat the layers of onion/honey or sugar, until all the onion slices are used up.
5. Put a china plate over the top of the bowl and leave for a day.
6. The onion and honey/sugar will produce a liquid as the onion juices mix in.
7. Take one dessertspoonful twice a day. *(You can take it more often if you wish but it could give you diarrhoea if you take too much! Only give it to children over the age of 5 and give 2 TEASPOONS every day)*
8. What you have made should last for a week. But if you run out of liquid, just make another batch with fresh ingredients.

NOTE: You can add crushed garlic to this mixture if you wish. (DO NOT TAKE ONION SYRUP IF YOU ARE BREASTFEEDING)

PLANTS YOU CAN ADD TO YOUR SYRUP

PLANT	PARTS USED	BENEFIT
Angelica	Leaves and stems	Decongestant
Echinacea	Fresh flowers	Anti-viral, soothing
Elder	Cooked berries (never raw) and flowers	Anti-viral, soothing
Flax	Crushed seeds	Expectorant
Goji	Berries	Anti-viral, soothing
Hollyhock	Fresh flowers	Soothing
Honeysuckle	Fresh flowers	Anti-inflammatory, soothing
Lavender	Dried flowers	Antiseptic
Marjoram	Leaves	Antiseptic, decongestant
Marshmallow	Leaves and flowers	Decongestant, soothing
Nasturtium	Fresh flowers	Decongestant
Pansy	Fresh flowers	Decongestant
Rosehips	Fresh berries	Anti-viral, soothing
Sage	Leaves	Decongestant
Thyme	Leaves	Antiseptic, expectorant
Violet	Fresh flowers	Anti-inflammatory, calming

Steam *inhalations*

Breathing in gentle steam from a bowl of water is an ancient remedy for clearing the sinuses and loosening catarrh in the chest. The addition of plants to the bowl of hot water can add more effectiveness to the treatment.

Boil a kettle of water and pour it into a plastic bowl. Add your chosen plants (crush them a little) and let them steep for a few minutes to release their fragrances. Put a towel over your head and lean over the bowl, breathing in and out as deeply as you can. It may make you cough a little. Some of the plants, we have suggested below, are considered to be expectorants (in other words they loosen a congested chest). You may need to wipe your face occasionally with the towel because of steam dripping off your face! This can be repeated daily until the congestion/blocked sinuses are better. It is particularly useful before bedtime, to aid restful sleep, so we have included a few sleep-inducing plants in the list below. You can mix the plants in your steam inhalation.

PLANTS	PARTS TO USE	PROPERTIES
Anise	Crushed seed pod	Expectorant
Eucalyptus	Leaves	Decongestant
Holy basil	Leaves	Antimicrobial
Horehound	Flowers, leaves	Antimicrobial, expectorant
Hyssop	Flowers, leaves	Antiseptic
Lavender	Flowers (fresh or dried)	Calming, sleep aid
Lungwort	Leaves	Expectorant, decongestant
Mint (all types)	Leaves	Decongestant
Oregano	Leaves	Antiseptic
Passionflower	Leaves	Calming, sleep aid
Sage	Leaves	Anti-inflammatory
Scots Pine	Dried needles	Antiseptic, sleep aid
Spruce	Dried needles	Antiseptic, sleep aid
Thyme	Flowers, leaves	Antiseptic, expectorant
Violet	Flowers (fresh)	Anti-inflammatory, sleep-aid

Mouthwashes

There are lots of plants that have antiseptic, antibacterial and microbial elements that you can make into a very effective mouthwash (that doesn't contain lots of chemicals). Also, many people (particularly the elderly) find commercial mouthwashes rather harsh for sensitive gums. We offer two alternatives here.

A basic mouthwash would be a decoction of herbs, to which you add 1 teaspoon of baking soda. It all depends which flavour you like! It is recommended that you make a fresh batch each week, as it will not keep beyond that. Please note that mouthwashes should be rinsed around the mouth and spat out. Do not swallow them (particularly the alcohol-based one).

MAKING A DECOCTION

2ozs (50g) dried plants, crushed with a mortar and pestle

2 pints (1.2 litre) water

1. Put the plants and water into a stainless steel or enamel pan.
2. Bring to the boil and then simmer for about fifteen minutes.
3. Strain through a fine sieve.
4. Return the liquid to a clean pan and simmer again, without a lid, to reduce the mixture by half by evaporation. Watch the pan carefully to make sure you don't reduce it too much.
5. Allow to cool before adding any other ingredients.

Mouthwash 1

Add to the decoction: 1 teaspoon of baking soda; 1 teaspoon of honey (Manuka if you can get it), then pour the liquid into a sterilised bottle and label with the ingredients used and how to use it. (E.g. Do not dilute. Use twice a day.)

MAKING A TINCTURE

NOTE: A mouthwash made with a tincture should NOT be gifted to a household with children, as it is strong alcohol.

1. In a large jam jar, with a lid, put 2ozs (50g) dried plants and cover with ½pint (300ml) vodka.
2. Put the lid on and store in it a cool, dark cupboard for two weeks.
3. After that period, strain through a sieve. The resulting liquid is now a tincture and needs to be diluted as below to make a mouthwash.

Mouthwash 2

Make a tisane (tea-type drink) with some more plant matter – about 5 teaspoons of dried plant and pour over boiling water. Not too much water. If you make the tisane in a teapot that is big enough for four people, that should be sufficient. Let the tisane 'brew' for about five minutes and cool a little, then pour ½pint (300ml) , through a sieve, into a measuring jug. Add 1 teaspoon of honey (runny). Combine this liquid with the alcohol based tincture, give it a very vigorous stir, so that everything is combined thoroughly. Bottle (probably in several bottles), label with ingredients and gift. This mouthwash will keep several months because of the alcohol element.

SUGGESTED PLANTS FOR MOUTHWASHES

(You can mix the type of plants. Experiment with flavours!)

PLANT	PARTS USED	BENEFITS
Caraway	Crushed dried seeds	Breath freshener
Fennel	Crushed dried seeds	Breath freshener
Horsetail	All except roots	Antibacterial, anti-inflammatory
Hyssop	Flowers and leaves	Antiseptic
Ladies Mantle	Fresh flowers	Good for inflamed and bleeding gums
Lovage	Flowers and leaves	Anti-microbial, anti-inflammatory
Marigold	Fresh flowers	Good for inflamed and bleeding gums
Mint	Dried or fresh leaves	Breath freshener, anti-bacterial
Oregano	Flowers and leaves	Breath freshener, antiseptic
Quince	Fresh fruit and leaves	Good for mouth ulcers
Spearmint	Dried or fresh leaves	Breath freshener, anti-bacterial
Thyme	Flowers and leaves	Breath freshener, antiseptic

A basic tooth powder

Bicarbonate of soda is the base for any tooth powder (which you use in place of toothpaste). You can add some pink Himalayan salt as well, which is antiseptic and good for the gums. Add some herbs and spices for flavouring and you will have a unique and natural cleanser that will make a fine gift.

BASIC RECIPE

7oz (175g) bicarbonate of soda

1oz (25g) Pink Himalayan salt or white sea salt

1 teaspoon of dried sage

1 teaspoon of dried mint or spearmint

Grind everything into a fine powder, put it in a brown glass jar or plastic pot with a screw top and label with the ingredients and the instructions to 'moisten your toothbrush, dip it in the powder and brush your teeth!'

Eye health

Anything that you put on the fragile skin under and around your eyes will filter straight through to your sinuses. So, if you have a headache caused by irritated sinuses, or irritated eyes due to staring at a screen for too long, or because it's the hayfever season, then you could try the following:

1. Smooth aloe vera gel, fresh from the plant, under your eyes. If you want to gift it then you need to add some Vitamin E oil (1 teaspoon to every 2 tablespoons of fresh gel) and whizz it up in a blender. Put into sterilised jars and keep in the fridge until gifted. Advise the recipient to keep it in the fridge as well.

2. Blend some cucumber slices, a little plain yoghurt and a teaspoon of honey (Manuka preferably) spread the mixture around your eyes and lay down for a rest. Remove with damp cotton wool. If you gift this, in a sterilised pot, advise that it should be refrigerated and used fairly quickly.

3. The plant eyebright, as its name suggests, has been used for centuries in salves and washes for eyes. The safest way to use it is to pour boiling water (about a mugful) over the dried or fresh flowers and leaves. Leave to infuse and cool. Then soak a plain cotton eye mask in the liquid and place over your closed eyes whilst you rest. Instead of eyebright, you could use fennel seeds, chamomile flowers or parsley.

Bath salts

The best thing about bath salts is that they contain a hefty dose of magnesium, which is so good for every process in the body and very, very relaxing. Having said that, DO NOT GIFT THESE TO ANYONE WHO IS PREGNANT – some essential oils and too much magnesium can be harmful. Also, because Epsom salts have such a sedative effect when put in a bath, it is probably best not to add to that effect by using any of the essential oils or plants that also have a sedative effect, like lavender, chamomile. Try the citrus fragrances, or others, such as sandalwood or rose.

Making your own bath salts ensures that everything is natural. You can even source natural food colourings to give the salts a gorgeous hue.

HOW TO MAKE BATH SALTS

4ozs (100g) coarse sea salt

4ozs (100g) bicarbonate of soda (baking soda but NOT baking powder)

1lb (450g) Epsom salts

About one dessertspoonful of essential oil (fragrance or mixture of fragrances are your choice)

2ozs (50g) of dried aromatic leaves, petals, buds and herbs of your choice.

Food colouring.

Stir together the baking soda and salts in a dry bowl. Drizzle a little food colouring over the bowl contents and mix thoroughly. Keep adding colouring until you get the shade that you want. Then add about 10-15 drops of fragrance. Finally, stir in the natural plant pieces, put into glass or plastic containers, decorate (a ribbon perhaps?) and gift.

Bath bombs

These perfumed and colourful bath bombs will fizz into a bath giving it a lovely perfume. They are very easy to make but you have to work quickly. Any water added to the basic mixture will cause it to start fizzing and melting. But if you compress it quickly into moulds, this action will stop, and it will start to dry. It is a great way to use dried plants, flowers and herbs from your garden and the ingredients are easy to source from craft shops in the high street or online. *NOTE: DO NOT GIFT TO ANYONE WHO IS PREGNANT.*

HOW TO MAKE BATH BOMBS

10ozs (250g) sodium bicarbonate • 4ozs (100g) granular citric acid

About one dessertspoonful of essential oil of your choice • Natural food colourings

About 2ozs (50g) of small pieces of dried aromatic herbs, leaves and flowers.

1. Put the two powdered substances in a dry bowl. Add the essential oil and work quickly, to make sure the oil is evenly mixed in.
2. Then add the food colouring, a little at a time, working it in with your hands. Add the plant pieces. Now, run a bowl of cold water, ready to dip your hands in when needed.
3. So, with slightly wet hands, pick up a clump of the mixture and roll it lightly around in your palms. It should squeeze together, like dough, in your hands. Press it into your chosen mould. Individual silicone moulds for little cakes – hearts or flower shapes work well.
4. Leave them to dry for a day, peel the silicone moulds off and wrap each bath bomb tightly in cling film, to keep them dry. Gift them in baskets, bowls or sealed containers.

Hair oils

Most substances that we apply to our hair are, in fact, acting upon the scalp, to clean it, nourish it and heal it from problems like dandruff. Although, obviously, any oil applied to the hair will also make the hair shine. But many infused oils that you can put on your scalp, will also have added health benefits such as inducing relaxation, aiding sleep and so on. The plant aromas of the oil are just as important as the oil itself (see the table opposite). It is so simple to make these oils from plants from your garden.

How to use them

Hair oils should be massaged into your scalp (only a little each time), brushing through to the ends of the hair, several hours before shampooing your hair. If possible, wrap warm towels around your head, or wear a shower cap to aid absorption. Some people prefer to put a towel over their pillow and leave the hair oil in overnight, showering it out in the morning.

What type of oil?

Use a light oil for applying to the hair and scalp, not a sticky, heavy oil. Oils such as grapeseed; safflower; sunflower; jojoba; argan or warmed coconut oil. You can add the contents of about three Evening Primrose or Vitamin E capsules to the mixture. They are natural preservatives and give the hair oil a little more shelf life. Only make small quantities at a time. One small bottle should last you for three or four applications at one a week.

RECIPE FOR ROSEMARY OIL

To clear the mind, aid concentration, alleviate fatigue and clear sinuses.

2ozs (50g) dried rosemary leaves

½ pint (300 ml) of your chosen oil

Contents of 3 Vitamin E oil capsules

METHOD

1. Put the oils and the rosemary leaves into a slow cooker on low or in a sealed casserole dish in a very low oven.
2. Cook for 3 hours.
3. Cool, strain and bottle.
4. When required, rub a little into the scalp and brush through to the hair ends.
5. If possible, leave in overnight, and wash out with shampoo in the morning.
6. Do not use a conditioner/shampoo combination or apply conditioner after washing.

Other useful plants for use in hair oils

Use the recipe given above, substituting other plants for the dried rosemary leaves. You can combine plants, but we suggest that you do not combine two plants that have a sedative action – unless you are going to go to bed after applying the oil. Do not apply any of these oil mixtures to cuts, grazes, open wounds or bleeding spots.

PLANT	WHICH PART	USEFUL FOR
Alfalfa	Flowers and leaves	Stimulates hair growth
Borage	Flowers and leaves	Menopause and mood lifting
Chamomile	Flowers	Anxiety and insomnia
Gardenia	Flowers	Anxiety and insomnia
Hops	Flowers	Sedative and anti-inflammatory
Juniper	Crushed berries	Anti-dandruff
Lavender	Dried flowers	Insomnia, anti-bacterial
Lemon Balm	Bruised leaves	Stress and tension
Oregano	Dried leaves	Anti-dandruff, anti-itch
Passion Flower	Dried flowers	Anxiety and insomnia
Silver Birch, weeping birch	Crushed bark	Anti-dandruff, hair growth

Hair Rinses

A rinse for the hair is best applied over a sink, with the plug in, so that it can be poured over the hair several times after the hair has been completely washed but not conditioned.

Applied cold, a hair rinse has a dual purpose. The cold water will tighten up the pores in the scalp and make the blood flow to the hair follicles, whilst whatever plants are added to the rinse will have other positive effects.

If you gift any of these rinses, then you must explain on the label the benefits of the rinse and how long it will keep. It is best stored in the refrigerator, used no more than once a week, and will keep for a month.

HOW TO MAKE A HAIR RINSE

Put two handfuls of bruised/torn fresh leaves or crushed flowers into a heatproof bowl. Pour over half a pint (300ml) of boiling water and leave to steep for a whole day, covering the bowl with a plate to keep the steam inside the bowl. When cold, strain the liquid into a jug, through a sieve, and add 2 tablespoons of white wine vinegar. Stir, bottle and label. Keep in the refrigerator until gifted.

SUGGESTED HAIR RINSES

PLANT	WHAT IT IS GOOD FOR
Chamomile flowers and juice of half lemon	Makes blonde hair lighter
Holy Basil (Tulsi) leaves and flowers	Anti-dandruff, thin hair, calming
Lavender flowers	Anti-dandruff
Marigold flowers and juice of half lemon	Makes blonde hair lighter also as an insect repellent (midges, mosquitoes)
Nettle leaves (wear rubber gloves to pick!)	Anti-dandruff and dry hair
Parsley leaves	Anti-dandruff
Pansy flowers	Anti-dandruff
Rosemary leaves	Conditions thin and dry hair
Sage leaves	Makes dark hair darker and glossier
Thyme leaves	Anti-bacterial, anti-dandruff
Yarrow flowers	To combat greasy hair

Perfumed Salves

Making a solid perfumed salve which also nourishes the skin is a wonderful gift to make for a friend who appreciates natural beauty products.

First you have to make your infused perfumed oil. Stick to one fragrance per bottle of oil, that way you will get a good scent and, hopefully, a good colour. Flowers that work really well for a fragranced oil are damask red rose petals, or lavender flowers, or marigold flowers. It is suggested that you keep your bottles of oil, infusing throughout the summer, in a greenhouse or conservatory, where they get plenty of sun.

Making infused perfumed oil

Basically, you need to take a three-quarters full large glass jar of vegetable oil, like sunflower or olive oil (don't use plastic containers because sunlight on plastic releases toxins, which you don't want in your lovely natural gift). Add a handful of your chosen flowers or petals and screw the lid on tightly. Put in a sunny place to infuse. When the flowers or petals turn brown (usually after about a week) pour the oil through a sieve and into a new glass jar, add fresh petals and screw the lid back on again. Do this every week until your source of fresh flowers or petals has gone. The oil should now be tinged with the colour of the flowers you have used and also contain the scent. You can add a few drops of purchased essential oil and a few drops of natural food colouring if you want a more intense scent and colour. (Sometimes, a lack of sun during the summer can produce a weaker scent on the flowers and also affect the infusion of the oil).

Making the salve

Put ½pint (300ml) of your infused oil in a heatproof bowl and add 1oz (25g) cosmetic grade beeswax pellets (available online). Put the bowl into a larger diameter saucepan and half-fill the saucepan with water (it should be well below the rim of the bowl containing the oil and beeswax. Bring the water to boiling point, whilst stirring the oil/beeswax mixture until the beeswax pellets melt. Take the bowl out of the saucepan and allow to cool just a little. At this point, if you wish to boost the colour, you could add half a teaspoon of a cosmetic grade mica powder (available online), stirring it thoroughly into the oil/beeswax mixture to evenly distribute the colour. Then pour the mixture into your salve jars. When the salve has cooled and set, then you can label the jars.

NOTE: Do not use perfumed salves on babies, young children or anyone with an auto-immune skin condition such as eczema or psoriasis. They should also not be used as a face cream but put on the pulse points, hands or feet to nourish and fragrance.

Looking after *hands and feet*

There are lots of natural products you can create to make your hands and feet silky smooth and to nourish and treat your nails.

Exfoliate and Nourish

Get rid of all the grime, dead skin and hard skin by first giving hands and feet a good scrub with an exfoliating treatment. Most organic manufacturers use natural products in their scrubs, such as crushed peach or apricot kernels but, without commercial grinders it is very difficult to crush hard fruit stones into fine particles. You are much safer using gritty sea salt or demerara sugar as a base for a scrub, with the addition of a perfumed infused oil (See page 53). Once the skin has been exfoliated, then you can nourish.

BASIC RECIPE FOR A SCRUB

4ozs (100g) rough salt (either sea or Himalayan) OR demerara sugar (rough granules)
2ozs (50g) infused scented oil
Optional: some dried herbs sprinkled in the mixture, such as rosemary, sage or mint.

Combine the ingredients in a bowl, mixing them together with a spoon.

To use the scrub on your hands, just scoop up a ball of the mixture in the palm of one hand and proceed to 'wash' both hands vigorously, front and palm, as though you were washing your hands. After working the mixture with your hands for at least two minutes, rinse off.

To use the scrub on your feet, lay down a towel, have a footbath ready at one side and put on rubber gloves. (This is so that continually working the gritty mixture over your feet doesn't make your fingertips sore). Then work the mixture over all the feet – heels and balls particularly – before rinsing off.

To give this as a gift, it would be best to give it in two containers. One for the salt or sugar with dried herbs mixture, another for the infused oil. Give instructions for mixing together and usage.

BASIC RECIPE FOR A MASK

A small raw, peeled and grated, potato OR mashed up contents of a lemon OR half a dozen mashed strawberries or raspberries OR mashed peach, apricot, nectarine or yellow fleshed plums.
(Do not be tempted to use any fruits that may stain your skin purple – like blackberries, blueberries, purple plums or mulberries!)
A teaspoon of honey (Manuka if possible)
2 teaspoons of a light facial oil, like Vitamin E or Jojoba
2 teaspoons of Greek style thick plain yoghurt.

Combine all the ingredients in a bowl. Spread it on to one hand and encase the hand in a clear plastic bag and put an elastic band around your wrist. Leave for half an hour then remove the plastic bag and wash your hand. Repeat with the other hand. Then do the same for your feet – one foot at a time, encased in a plastic bag, as you did with your hands. Hands and feet should feel silky smooth. Do it once a week for best effect. If you are gifting this to someone, gift it, fully mixed, on the day they are going to use it, accompanied by full instructions.

Treat your nails

You will need to purchase some glass roller ball bottles, new empty nail varnish bottles with brushes, or glass dropper bottles – all of which are available online very cheaply.

There are two types of treatment for nails. One is a remedial treatment for any nail problems, such as nail fungus, infections or whitlows. The other is a softening and nourishing treatment for your cuticles, which will help nails to grow.

Remedial oil

For the remedial treatment, you will need an infused oil. (See page 19). Plants that can be used in the infusion are as follows:

Thyme; Basil; Lemongrass; Mint (any type); Lavender; Marigold, Echinacea; St. John's Wort. All of them have antiseptic properties and may help to alleviate any fungal or infection problems. (Obviously if you have severe athlete's foot or a nail infection you will need to see a doctor).

Simply fill a small bottle with your chosen infused oil and then roll the ball (or paint or put a few drops) over your nails, paying particular attention to the sides. You can also use it in between your toes and apply every day if you wish. Store in a cool dark place (but not the fridge).

Cuticle oil

The purpose of this oil is to nourish and to also smell nice!
Therefore, the base of this treatment would be a perfumed infused oil (see page 53).
Using plants such as: scented dark roses, lavender, chamomile, jasmine, violet.

BASIC RECIPE FOR A CUTICLE OIL

2 teaspoons jojoba oil • 2 teaspoons Argan oil
Contents of 2 Vitamin E capsules
2 teaspoons scented infused oil
Add all the oils to the glass bottle. Seal shake vigorously and label. Apply to the cuticles of finger and toenails at least once a week and massage in. Store in a cool dark place (but not the fridge).

Lip balms

Nothing is worse than dry or cracked lips and this solid salve will be perfect to gift to friends. You can also colour them with natural edible food colourings and add natural food flavours, to improve the appearance, taste and smell. Shea butter and beeswax pellets can be bought online. You can also buy small lip balm pots or tins very cheaply online, which will enable you to make batches for several friends at once! We give you some options of infused oils, colours and flavours below.

BASIC RECIPE
4 fl.oz (100ml) infused oil (see Page 53) • 1½ oz (40g) beeswax pellets
1½ oz (40g) shea butter • Some edible food colouring • Some edible flavouring

1. Melt the beeswax and shea butter in a heatproof bowl over simmering water in a saucepan.
2. Remove the bowl, once the substances have melted and add the infused oil.
3. Add a few drops of colouring, stirring well until all the colour has combined thoroughly. Add more if you want an intense colour.
4. Add a few drops of the flavouring. Don't be tempted to add too much. 1 teaspoon should be plenty. Again, stir really well.
5. Pour the mixture into your tins or pots, filling to just below the rim. Leave to completely cool and solidify before you put on the lids. Label and gift!

SUGGESTIONS FOR COMBINATIONS

Infused oil	Colour	Flavour
Calendula (marigold)	Yellow	Sicilian Lemon
Calendula (marigold)	Orange	Valencian Orange
Elderflowers	No colour or pale yellow	Elderflower or Pineapple or Sicilian Lemon
Mint	Green	Mint extract
Rose	Pink or Red	Rose flavouring or Raspberry
Spearmint	Green or Blue	Spearmint

Basically, you can do all sorts of combinations – play around!

Face Masks

There are many types of face masks, but we are going to concentrate on three options here – a clay-based mask that tones and draws out impurities in the skin; a yoghurt-based mask that nourishes the skin; and a mashed fruit/vegetable or plant mask that does the job of revitalising or healing the skin.

Types of clay for masks (available online)

Australian pink clay or Rhassoul clay – *good for all skin types – especially elderly skin.*
Moroccan red clay, Bentonite clay or Fuller's Earth clay – *good for acne or oily skin.*
French Green clay – *oily to normal skin, or combination skin.*
Fuller's Earth clay – *lightens darker skin*
White Kaolin clay – *sensitive or allergy prone skin*

HERB WATERS TO BE ADDED TO CLAY MASKS (see opposite)

PLANT	PARTS USED	BENEFIT
Chamomile	Flowers (fresh or dried)	Moisturising, anti-inflammatory
Mallow	Flowers and leaves	Moisturising, anti-inflammatory
Olive	Leaves	Anti-inflammatory
St. John's Wort	Flowers	Soothes sunburn
Witch Hazel	Dried bark, twigs, leaves	Astringent, anti-acne

BASIC CLAY MASK RECIPE

4 tablespoons of clay powder

2.5 fl.ozs (80ml) herb/plant water *(made by simmering your chosen crushed plant in water for 15 minutes, then straining to remove the plant matter.)*

2 tablespoons of infused oil *(see page 19 or 53)*

Mix everything together and apply to the face and/or neck and chest, leaving the area around the eyes clear. This mask will harden. Leave on the skin for 15 minutes if you have dry skin, 30 minutes if you have oily skin.

In order to gift this mask, you will need to give the recipient three pots/bottles – one of powdered clay, one of infused water and one of infused oil. Of course, you will also need to gift them the instructions regarding mixing them into a face mask. Only gift enough for 2 masks and suggest that the infused water is kept in the fridge.

Yoghurt-based mask

This recipe you can whizz up in a blender and gift it ready-made, but with instructions to keep it in the fridge.

Recipe

½pt (300ml) thick Greek style live yoghurt
3ozs (75g) oats
3 tablespoons hot water
1 teaspoon honey (Manuka if possible, otherwise organic)
6 large strawberries, cut up

1. Put the tablespoons of hot water in a small bowl and add the oats. Mash them into the water until it turns cloudy.
2. Add the oats and oat water, honey, strawberries and yoghurt to a blender and whizz into a thick cream.
3. Pot up in a sterilised glass jar with lid, label as a face pack, the date it was made, instructions to keep in the fridge and to use within two weeks.
4. Instructions for use: Cover the face with a hot flannel to open the pores. Apply a thick layer of the cold face mask (obviously this mask won't harden). Leave on for 30 minutes, then wash off with warm water. Do not apply any face cream for at least a couple of hours.

Mashed fruit, vegetable or plant masks

People pay a lot of money for expensive creams and serums that contain fruit acids and plant extracts, which are supposed to remove dead skin and brighten up the new skin underneath. Many plants can be applied straight to the skin, but do not apply any fruit or plant substance to broken skin, wounds or bleeding spots, to be on the safe side. You need to apply these masks whilst lying down on a towel. They are liable to slip off if you are sitting or standing, and they are a bit messy!

PLANTS	WHAT TO DO	BENEFIT
Aloe Vera	Cut open leaves and scrape out gel. Apply to skin and leave for one hour.	Healing and soothing, Good for sunburn, eczema and allergic skin reactions.
Chamomile	A handful of dried flowers. Put in a blender with 2 tablespoons almond oil. Apply gunge to skin and leave for 20 minutes.	Anti-inflammatory and anti-bacterial
Cucumber	Remove skin and mash. Apply straight to skin.	Soothing and hydrating for dry and inflamed skin
Pelargoniums (scented variety)	Blend a handful of leaves with 2 teaspoons of Manuka or organic honey.	Reviving and healing. Soothing scents are relaxing.
Strawberries	Hull and mash, adding 2 teaspoons of lemon juice. Only leave on face for 20 minutes.	High fruit acid to brighten and renew skin.

Cheat's *liquid Soap*

Making hard soap is complicated, as it requires using chemicals, like lye, which can be dangerous to use. You can, of course, buy 'melt and pour' kits for hard soap but it is difficult to add extra ingredients to those, as any additional oils or fats will prevent them from setting. So, we are suggesting a sneaky recipe for liquid soap, to which you can add your own infused water and oil, colouring and perfume. We suggest that you either stick to one plant for the infused water and oil (like elderflower or lavender) or you combine some herbs that go well together (like rosemary, basil and thyme). You can buy glass or plastic refillable pump bottles online. It would also be useful to have a small plastic funnel for pouring into the bottles easily.

Note: We suggest that you don't use food processors or blenders for this recipe, as they can be difficult to fully clean sometimes, and you don't want your baking tasting of soap for weeks to come.

RECIPE

A basic bar of soap (ivory or white with little or no perfume)
1 tsp glycerine • ½pt (300ml) infused water (see No.2 below) • 2 fl.oz (60ml) infused argan oil (see pages 19 & 53) • Natural food colouring • Essential oil (optional)

1. Grate the bar of soap into a large glass or Pyrex bowl.
2. Boil ½pt (300ml) of water and pour it over your chosen dried herbs/flowers/plants in a separate bowl. Leave to infuse for half an hour. Strain and set liquid aside.
3. In a saucepan, boil the infused water again, then pour it over the soapflakes, leaving them to melt, then whip the mixture quickly with a whisk or handheld mixer until it resembles paste.
4. Add the glycerine, infused oil and colouring and whip again until it is a consistent colour and texture. You can add some extra scent by adding a few drops of essential oil, if you wish. Bottle and label.

Insect *repellents*

There are certain scents that insects dislike and you can use them to protect your skin and your vegetable and fruit plants. So you could gift potted plants with an explanation of how they keep insects at bay and where they could be planted, or you could gift a plant scented water or oil spray for skin. Some plants can be used straight on to the skin – lemon balm, mint or thyme leaves, for example, which can be crushed and rubbed on to the skin. A large pot of lavender, for example, can be placed on a patio table to keep gnats, midges and mosquitos at bay. Crysanthemums appear to be a super repellent! And anything that smells of lemon keeps biting insects away!

So, to recap, you could give gifts in the following form:

1. Potted plants to use as insect repellents on the patio, in the garden or in the house.
2. Make sachets of dried lavender or any of the lemon-scented plants, for your recipient to make their own scented water to use on their skin.
3. Make an infused oil for rubbing into the skin (See page 19).
4. Make an infused water for spraying on the skin. (Just like making tea but leave it steep for quite a while to get the full aroma. Dried plants are often more powerful).

PLANT	REPELS	USAGE
Bay	Flies	Have it in pots by doorways and a small one in the kitchen.
Basil	Flies, Mosquitoes, Thrips	Leaves can be rubbed on the skin, keep a plant in the kitchen, make an infused water spray for plants.
Borage	Tomato hornworms, Cabbage worms	Plant near tomato plants and cabbages.
Catnip	Flea beetles, Ants, Japanese beetles, Weevils	Catnip infused water can be poured on ant's nests, sachets of dried catnip can be hung in fruit trees and on climbing veg, like runner beans etc. But beware! It will attract cats! You may prefer another plant deterrent.
Chives	Japanese beetles, Carrot flies	Plant near carrots and roses.
Chrysanthemum	Ants, Cockroaches, Japanese beetles, Spider mites, Ticks, Silverfish, Harlequin bugs, Lice	Plants can be used anywhere in patio or garden or near a dog's bed.
Garlic	Root maggots, Carrot root flies, Codling moths, Aphids	Plant anywhere in the veg and fruit garden. NOT recommended that you rub it into your skin but you could put a saucer of crushed garlic in oil on your patio table when you sit out there. A garlic water infusion can be sprayed on plants infested with aphids.

PLANT	REPELS	USAGE
Lavender	Gnats Midges Mosquitoes Fleas Moths	Plant around a patio where people sit out and eat. Can be used on the skin in creams, water sprays and infused oils. DON'T be tempted to rub the flowers into your dog's fur or spray your dog's bed with lavender water. Lavender contains linalool, which is toxic for dogs and cats.
Lemon balm Lemon basil Lemon beebalm Lemon catmint Lemon eucalyptus Lemongrass Lemon mint Lemon myrtle Lemon scented geraniums Lemon thyme Lemon verbena	Gnats Midges Mosquitoes	There are also some cultivars of roses, magnolias or irises which have lemon-scented flowers. Ideal for planting around patios and garden ponds to keep biting insects at bay. Some of these lemon-scented plants listed have leaves that can be rubbed straight on to the skin. All of them will make quite strong water or oil infusions for spraying on the skin.
Marigold	Lice Mosquitoes Aphids Thrips Whiteflies Tomato Hornworms	Scented marigolds (the leaves) can be rubbed on on the skin but many people do not like their strong, odd scent. Their greatest use is as an insect repellent in the vegetable garden. Pots of marigolds can keep biting insects at bay if placed on your outside tables.
Mint (all types)	Spiders Ants Mosquitoes	Can all be rubbed on the skin. Make a mint tea and and use it, when cooled, as a skin spray. Infuse oil with mint and use on the skin. Grow mint in pots, by the back door, to stop ant invasions. It is best to only grow mint in pots as it is very invasive. Spray a strong mint tea on ant nests and garden infestations. Hang used mint tea bags in your fruit trees and bushes to deter ants and spiders.

SECTION 3 : *Crafts*

Preserving flowers and foliage

Preserving some of the more beautiful flowers in your garden, to give as everlasting bouquets or to use in crafts, is an excellent idea.

Flowers should ideally be harvested when in full bud or they have just fully opened. They should be cut in the middle of a dry and sunny day, when the flowers have their face to the sun, all the morning dew has disappeared, and they have not yet begun to flag in the afternoon heat. The flower heads should be perfect and without blemish. Only pick flowers with long stems. Short flowers like pansies, are best used as pressed flowers. Foliage should be equally perfect and not curled up with lack of water or nutrients.

There are several ways of drying flowers and foliage. Below the explanation of each method, we give some suggestions as to which flowers seem to respond better to that particular method of drying.

Air drying

This is the traditional method if you want to create bouquets and posies or floral hearts, swags or wreath arrangements. This is simply the technique of binding them in to bunches and hanging the flowers/foliage upside down from a pole or wire in the middle of a dark dry room, such as an outhouse/shed/storeroom or spare bedroom. The air must be able to circulate around the bunches and the atmosphere must be completely dry. Therefore, do not be tempted to dry them in a kitchen or bathroom, where water and steam are present on a regular basis – and do not attempt to dry flowers/foliage in garden buildings during a spell of damp weather. Don't forget that some stems may shrink as they dry, so it best to use elastic bands or elasticated string to bind the bunches, which will shrink with the stems. Providing the conditions are right, air-drying can take up to ten days to complete. Then turn them right way up and put them into dry empty vases until you are ready to create your gift.

FLOWERS/FOLIAGE SUITABLE FOR AIR DRYING

Allium; Astilbe; Chrysanthemum; Dahlia; Delphinium; Dianthus; Echinacea; Goldenrod; Gypsophilia; Lavender; Love-in-a-Mist; Marigold; Mugwort; Peony; Rose; Sages; Wormwood; Yarrow; Zinnia.

Drying with a desiccant

This method is usually used for just the flower heads, when they are to be used for inserting into wreaths, posies and balls, (see page 93) or to be used when making acrylic jewellery or paperweights (see page 76). If you are drying the heads with a view to wiring them into a wreath or other display, then it is best to put wire around the top of the stem before you cut off the length of the stem (leaving about ½inch(1cm) below the flower head) and before you place the flower heads in a desiccant. The most common drying medium is silica gel, which can be bought very easily online. You don't want the little bags, often found tucked in shoes and other items bought online, you want a large bag of either the silica crystals, gel or silica sand. There are further refinements, such as silica gel that changes colour when it has absorbed all the moisture from the plants, and silica gel that can be re-used over and over again by drying it out in a microwave oven.

The technique is quite simple. Half- fill a biscuit tin, plastic box or some other container with a lid, with the silica, then gently place the flowers, spaced out, stalk down into the desiccant. Then gently, with a spoon, sprinkle dessicant over the flower heads, trying to get as much inside the petals as possible. Make a little mound of desiccant over each flower, so that you know where they are. Put the lid on the container and leave it alone. Drying times vary, depending upon the size of the flowers but a good yardstick is a flower that is 1 inch (2cms) or less in diameter will dry in about 2 full days. Big flower heads can take up to 5 days. Sprays – like lilac – can be up to a week. Keep checking because you don't want them to get too dry and brittle. Remove from the desiccant very carefully. Store in a different box until ready to use. You should put a thin layer of silica gel in the bottom just to guard against any damp.

FLOWER HEADS SUITABLE FOR DRYING IN DESICCANT

Carnation; Daffodil (leave stem on); Dahlia; Delphinium; Hollyhock; Hyacinth (leave stem on); Larkspur; Lilac (leave stem on); Marigold; Meadowsweet; Peony; Rose; Queen-of-the Forest; Queen of the Prairie; Sunflower (small varieties); Tulip; Zinnia.

Oven Drying

This would be the same as drying any other plants. Set the oven at its lowest possible temperature and place the flowers (with stems if you wish) on a double layer of greaseproof paper on a baking tray. A quantity of small flowers (like lavender) may only take half an hour to dry but larger flowers will take longer. It's a question of checking often.

Microwave ovens can be used but, even on their lowest setting, they can be quite fierce, so the recommendation is that you use larger flowers and try drying them in short bursts of thirty seconds at a time. Oven drying is suitable for the types of flowers mentioned under air-drying.

Using Glycerine

This is the best way of preserving sprays of tiny flowers and leaves, such as gypsophilia (baby's breath) mimosa and ferns.

Remove lower leaves from the stems and crush the ends, as though you were putting them in a vase arrangement. Then stand them in a large vase and pour in 2 pints (1.2 litre) of boiled and cooled (but still hot) water (to which a tablespoon of salt had been added). Leave for one full day and then remove from the salty water, which you can discard. Then put the sprays into a fresh vase, to which you add 1 pint (600ml) hot water, in which has been mixed ½pint (300ml) glycerine. The process of the plants absorbing the glycerine this way will take from 1 week to 10 days, during which time they will get darker and glossier. Remove and place in an empty, dry vase until needed.

To preserve individual leaves, using the glycerine method, lay the leaves (with a short stalk still attached) in the bottom of a shallow flat pan, like a silicon cake shape. Mix one part glycerine with two parts hot water (no salt), mix thoroughly and pour over the leaves. To make sure that the leaves don't just float to the surface, keep them down by putting a slightly smaller metal pan or china dish into the solution on top of the leaves. Leave them to absorb the liquid for about 3 days. Then remove the leaves and dry them gently with kitchen paper.

PLANTS SUITABLE FOR GLYCERINE PRESERVATION

Baby's Breath; Bells of Ireland (sometimes known as Shell Flower); Eucalyptus; sprays of Ferns; Holly and Ivy sprays; Hop sprays; Lady's Mantle; twigs of autumn leaves such as Maple or Oak; Mimosa; Seed heads from Clematis and Foxglove.
Any individual leaves.

What can you create with dried flowers?

Bouquets are an obvious answer: However, the slightly muted colours of dried flowers suggest that you should gift them in a rustic vase or container, rather than wrapped in paper. Try looking around charity/thrift or secondhand shops to find something unusual. Meanwhile, there are lots of other options for making creative use of your dried flowers and foliage.

Baskets and China

There is nothing more lovely than doing an arrangement of dried flowers in a basket or trug. Again, you could try and source a small cheap basket from a charity shop or garden centre. Baskets can be easily painted in a bright colour, if it is stained or grubby. Broken bits of weaving can be superglued, or a ribbon can be glued around the defects. A presentation alternative for a dried flower arrangement can be a pretty piece of china – from a vintage teacup to a stylish teapot or an old chamber pot. They can all provide a unique and thoughtfully presented gift.

A display dome

Display a single dried flower or a small bouquet of flowers under a display dome. The Victorians were very fond of doing this. They are plentiful online and are sometimes called Glass Cloche Bells, Cake Display Domes, Display Globes or Bell Jar Domes and come in all sorts of sizes and exotic shapes. The easiest way to display dried plants in these display domes is to fix the stems into a small piece of oasis floral foam (the dry type) or a small polystyrene circle which is superglued to the base of the dome. (You may want to cover the foam or polystyrene piece first with some fabric or paper that makes it look more attractive, if you are displaying a single flower rather than a low arrangement that would cover up the base.)

Wreaths, Posies, Swags and other decorations

These uses of dried flowers and foliage are covered, to some extent, on pages 24 to 29, in the section on Christmas. The beauty of taking the time to preserve some of your best flowers and foliage is that whatever time of year gifts or decorations are required for an occasion, you won't be limited by what is available in your garden during that period.

Epoxy resin objects

First, let's make this simple. Epoxy resin can be made into art objects or jewellery (see page 76) that look like clear glass but weigh considerably less – and you can insert plants into the moulds and enclose them in the resin to make stunning objects, like paperweights, chunky key fobs, coasters, small bowls etc. But...and this is an important but...you need to buy the Hard Type Ultraviolet Curing Resin, which requires no complicated mixing or measuring, and it hardens by being exposed to sunlight or UV light. And you will need to buy some silicone moulds for whatever it is that you want to make. They come in all shapes and sizes, from tiny earring moulds to large wall plaques. You can also get inexpensive resin-curing UV lamps and torches online, but sunlight will do just as well. You will need a cheap small plastic measuring jug.

MOULDING RESIN

Measure the resin into the measuring jug, then slowly pour half of it into the mould. Pause and insert your dried flower/s, then continue to slowly fill the mould. Don't rush, or pour from too far away, otherwise you will create bubbles. Put the mould under a UV lamp or out in full sunlight for the specified number of minutes. (The resin will produce heat and a little gas, which quickly disperses). Remove the object from the mould and use an emory board or fine sandpaper to remove any rough edges. All done.

Potpourri

This is the perfect use for your dried, scented flowers and leaves. Dry potpourri is easy to make and, when placed in open bowls, will fill a room with a subtle perfume, which should last for several weeks before needing to be refreshed.

You could choose to blend a variety of scented dried flowers/ buds/ petals and aromatic leaves, or you could pick just one – like lavender or rose.

HOW TO MAKE A SIMPLE POTPOURRI

You need a pair of disposable latex gloves because you have to mix essential oils into the dried plant pieces by hand. You also need to purchase some orris root powder. This is a fixative and available from craft shops or online. Then you will need some essential oils of your choice – these can be bought online or from health food shops or pharmacies.

BASIC RECIPE

8ozs (200g) dried flowers/ buds/ petals/ leaves
2ozs (50g) orris root powder
6 drops in total of your chosen essential oil or oils.
1oz (25g) powdered cinnamon and/or nutmeg (optional)
(Some people like to add dried pieces of citrus peel or small aromatic fir cones.)

Put all dry ingredients -Plants/fixative/spices into a dry and sealable container (zip plastic bag or plastic lidded box). Seal and gently tumble the contents around for a couple of minutes. Do this every day for about a week.

Then unseal, add the essential oil/s, mixing into the dried material with gloved hands. Seal the container again and leave undisturbed for at least two weeks in a cool, dark place (not the fridge).

Then decant into your chosen display bowl or bowls. You could gift it in a bowl or in bags or sachets so that your recipients can decant it into their own bowl.

Pressed flowers

Probably the most pleasurable way of preserving flowers and foliage from your garden and the most versatile when it comes to using them in crafts. The best flowers to choose are the ones with delicate blooms and petals. The chunkier and showy flowers are better dried in bunches for 3D displays of preserved flowers.

The first thing you will need is a flower press. Wooden presses are quite reasonable in price and come in all sorts of sizes. You basically unscrew them, place your flowers that you have picked (on a dry sunny day when the blooms have shed any dew and are fully open) in between absorbent paper like toilet paper, kitchen paper or blotting paper, sandwich that between sheets of cardboard and screw the press down again. Alternatively, you can put the flowers between absorbent paper at the back of a large, heavy book, or between paper and card with a heavy weight on top. A flower press is probably the best way. Also, I personally prefer absorbent paper that has no patterns/quilting on it, as the pattern can transfer to the flowers. Keep your flower press or pressing system in a dry place in your house. Anywhere damp will seriously impede the process.

Change the absorbent paper after about a week and you should find that fragile flowers will be dry after two to three weeks. Just touch them with your finger. If they feel cold, then they still have moisture in them.

Once they are dry, you will want to store them somewhere until you are ready to use them. Totally dry plastic containers with lids, away from sunlight, and with the addition of packets of silica gel desiccant (very cheap online and re-useable) to keep everything dry.

There are so many fabulous crafts in which you can use pressed flowers and foliage and some are explained in the following pages.

THE BEST FLOWERS TO PICK FOR PRESSING

FLOWER	WHEN IT IS AT ITS BEST
Aconites (winter)	Winter
African Lily	Summer
Alliums	Spring
Amaranthus	Summer
Astilbe	Summer
Begonias	Summer
Bluebell	Spring
California Poppies	Summer
Canna Lilies	Summer
Catmint	Summer
Cherry blossom (winter)	Winter
Crocus	Autumn/Winter/Spring
Cyclamen	Winter
Daisies	Spring/Summer
Freesia	Spring
Gladiolus murielae	Autumn
Glory of the Snow	Winter
Heathers	Winter
Hellebores	Winter
Hibiscus	Summer
Japanese quince	Winter
Jasmine (winter)	Winter
Lavender	Summer
Lilac	Spring
Lily of the Valley	Spring
Nerine	Autumn
Pansies	Most of the year
Petunias	Summer
Russian snowdrop	Winter/Spring
Snowdrop	Winter
Sternbergia	Autumn
Viburnum	Winter

What can you make with *pressed flowers?*

The world is your oyster! There are so many things that can be embellished with delicate pressed flower arrangements and larger arrangements can be simply a piece of beautiful artwork to frame and hang on the wall.

However you decided to utilise your pressed dried plants, you will need a couple of pairs of different length craft tweezers (or delicate cosmetic tweezers – the types used by beauticians to attach false eyelashes or small pieces of artwork to nails). Obviously, the flowers are so delicate and your hands, no matter how clean, can transfer sweat to the plant matter. Then you will need craft glue – the type that dries clear. Or you may prefer spray glue. For wall pictures, stationery, bookmarks etc. you will want to have a range of interesting papers and cards, in different colours. Some projects will need to have some coats of clear sealing varnish (either painted or sprayed on). Some projects will need to be sealed with transparent sticky backed plastic (like bookmarks or greetings cards/notelets). Plan out your project first and then acquire the materials.

Stationery

Pressed flowers look beautiful on handmade paper, or cards, notelets or bookmarks. But, perhaps, are too delicate and special to be sent through the post. Perhaps reserve them for special occasion greetings – like a landmark wedding anniversary – and give them to your recipient by hand, when you see them.

Cards, notelets and bookmarks really need to be protected by transparent sticky backed plastic, once you completed the embellishment with the delicate plant matter and any other material you may have added, like fabric or lace.

Pictures and other artwork

Pressed flower pictures can be whatever your selection of plants and your taste dictate. They can be bold, or delicate – vibrant or muted. Gently lay out your chosen plants on the background and decide on their position before you start glueing. Mistakes, once glued, are not easily rectified with such delicate materials.

Of course, you may choose to make artwork for displaying on the wall or mantelpiece using other materials – like wood or pebbles. The wood plaques displayed here have pressed flowers glued to them in exactly the same way as you would on paper. (More about using the wood in your garden to make gifts on pages 83 - 85). As these plaques are not covered by a layer of protective glass, as a picture on paper would be, then you would need to spray them with several coats of clear varnish, front and back.

The decorative pebbles shown here, meant to grace any flat surface in a home, have first been painted with several coats of matt white acrylic paint. Once dry, the pressed flowers and foliage have been glued in place, then the pebbles have been coated with several layers of varnish.

Jewellery

There is a huge amount of stuff out there (online and in craft shops) for you to create jewellery, of all types, with your pressed flowers. What you can create is almost limitless.

You can purchase, very cheaply, empty mini frames. These are enclosed frames intended for embroidery display – but you can just as easily insert a pressed flower on a piece of card and add a chain, for wearing as a pendant. Equally, there are myriads of blank pin button badges; stainless steel earring blanks (with full fixings to wear); cufflink blanks; pendant bases; blank stick pins (meant for corsages but equally useful for affixing an enclosed frame of pressed flowers as an extravagant hat pin or lapel display; blank metal or plastic buttons for you to attached tiny pressed flowers and cover with sticky back plastic or clear varnish.

Many of these 'blanks' can be matched up with a same-size glass cabochon (or flat-backed clear glass bead) to glue over the pressed flower or flowers that you have glued on to the blank. This will protect it and have a slight magnifying effect.

The other way to use pressed flowers in jewellery is to suspend them in resin. For a complete explanation on how to use resin see page 70. Moulds can be bought very cheaply online or in craft shops. You can make pendants, beads, earrings, rings, bangles – in fact anything that takes your fancy! Fabulous way to use pressed flowers, although, with larger pieces of jewellery, dried rather than pressed flowers might be more useful.

Seed Bombs, Balls, Mats and Tapes

Really useful gifts to give to someone who is just starting out as a gardener, are prepared seed packages that are truly easy to plant. You can prepare these seed-delivery packages using seed saved from plants in your garden.

Seed Bombs

A little messy to make but they are a great method of seed delivery. A friend once admired a patch of beautiful poppies in my garden, so I saved some seeds from them and made a seed bomb, to enable my friend to create her own patch!

HOW TO MAKE A SEED BOMB

½ cup of seeds (1 type or a variety)

2½ cups of fine compost

2 cups of powdered clay (buy online or in a craft shop – Fullers Earth is best)

Water

1. Mix the seeds, compost and clay together in the bucket and gradually add the water until it forms into a fairly solid mud.
2. Shape the mixture into balls (about the size of tennis balls).
3. Place on a piece of newspaper to dry. The clay will make them harden.
4. To gift them, wrap them in clingfilm and write instructions:
   "Throw the seed bomb forcefully into a clear patch of soil and it should break up. If it doesn't then hit it with the back of your spade and work the debris into the soil. Water in and leave to grow. Obviously water well in dry weather."

Seed Mats

These are a great gift for someone who lives in an apartment with, at most, a balcony, and therefore needs to grow everything in pots.

So, what you need to do is take a typical medium-sized flowerpot (say 6in (15cms) diameter), place it on a piece of blank paper and draw around the bottom. This circle gives you a template. Cut around the circle and place it on some sheets of strong kitchen paper. Lay out your kitchen paper circles on a plastic sheet. (Or you could use a silicon mat if you are lucky enough to have one.) Then coat the kitchen paper in thick flour and water glue.

SIMPLE FLOUR PASTE:

1 cup of plain flour, 1 cup of water. Mix together thoroughly to remove all lumps.

Whilst the thick glue is wet, place your chosen seeds, well-spaced, on the circles and leave them to dry. Then cover them with blank circles of greaseproof paper, for protection and put them in suitable sized envelopes – one for each seed mat, marked with the name of the seeds. Gift with instructions: *"Fill a 6in(15cms) pot with compost to 1 inch (2cms) below the rim. Lay the seed mat on top of the compost – seeds facing upwards – and cover with ½inch (1cm) compost. Water well. The glue will gradually dissolve, releasing the seeds. The kitchen paper will gradually decompose."*

Seed Tapes

Fabulous gift that saves a gardener the back breaking work of sowing seeds individually in a flower bed or trough.

Get some paper raffia ribbon (you can buy it online or from craft or florists shops). Or you can cut thick toilet or kitchen paper into strips. Cut the ribbon into 12 inch (30cms) lengths. Lay on a flat surface covered with a plastic sheet or tablecloth covered in a thin film of oil or grease (or use a silicon mat). Make the flour and water glue (see above) and spread it thickly on the tapes. Place your seeds at strategic intervals along the tape and leave to dry. Once dried, place carefully into large envelopes and mark on the envelope the type of seeds on the tapes and instructions on planting, before you gift them.

Seed Balls for Birds

These are lovely autumn or winter gifts for a friend who loves watching birds in the garden and a good way to use up sunflower, melon and squash seeds (and any small seeds in your stash that are maybe out of date for planting). You can also add crushed eggshells, but you need to bake them, before crushing, in a pre-heated high oven for about 10 minutes. You can also add small pieces of apple. The recipe is very simple. Just melt a standard 8ozs (200g) block of suet or lard (can be made from animal fat or vegetable fat) gently in a pan on the stove or in the microwave. Once the fat has melted, remove from the heat or microwave and add double the weight of seeds, eggshells and apple pieces. Mix them altogether. Once it has cooled and the fat is beginning to solidify again, either use an ice cream scoop to take some out and shape it into a ball, or use your hands (run your hands under the cold tap, dry and work quickly with the mixture to shape it, otherwise it will start melting again). Put the balls in the fridge on greaseproof paper to firm up, then tie string around them (crossways,twice) and hang them in the garden in a shady place, in case there is a burst of sunshine that might melt them.

INTERESTING IDEAS FOR SEED GIFTS

IN MEMORIAM

I once attended the funeral of a friend, who was an avid gardener all her life. Her family chose to give everyone at the funeral a decorated envelope full of seeds from her favourite plants, with an explanation that her family hoped that her friends would plant a corner of their garden 'In Memory' of her and her love of gardening.

PARTY FAVOURS

Children can be encouraged to grow things by being given a packet of easy to grow seeds, with instructions, as part of their party bag offerings at a birthday celebration. (But only include them in the party bags of children who are of an age to be able to read – otherwise they may open them and eat them!) Suggestions for starting a child's mini garden are cress seeds, peas shoots, microgreens, selection of mixed salad leaves, radishes or little globe carrots.

Indoor Gardens

Gifting from your garden does not just mean from your outside space but also from your indoor gardens in your greenhouse, conservatory, windowsill or porch.

Gifting to family members or friends with little or no outside space themselves, means that you have to be creative. What better than to create a small indoor garden for them? The following pages have some suggestions.

The Cactus Garden

This must be planted in an open container and displayed in a dry place with plenty of light. Cacti do not like humidity, so it is best not to display them in the kitchen, bathroom or damp porch. If you are a cactus grower you will know this but, of course, you need to provide the person receiving your gift with full instructions regarding display and care.

Choose a sturdy shallow dish with drainage holes for the garden – china or terracotta is best. Plastic can get too warm. Fill with specialist cactus potting soil, which is full of grit and sand and gives the good drainage that cactus like.

Fill it with the new plants you have propagated from your own cacti by taking offsets from parent plants in late spring or summer. The offsets should come from high up on the parent plant and be at least 2ins (5cms) long. Put the offsets to dry out in a colander or sieve in a dry place (not in the sun). Let them dry for several days. If the offsets already have visible roots then they can be planted straight away in the 'garden'. Those offsets that don't yet have roots need to be planted in small pots of sand and charcoal mixture until some roots develop.

Once your cactus garden is planted up, and the surface is covered in plain or coloured gravel, wait for one week before watering.

SUGGESTED SMALL CACTI

Star cacti *(Astrophytum)* look like stars when viewed from above. There are several types and they usually produce yellow flowers.

Pincushion cacti *(Mammilaria)* look like their folk name suggests and grow often in mounds. Flowers can be white or purple.

Globular cacti have small globe-like bodies. They have names like Golden Ball or Hedgehog and the flowers can come in all colours.

There are so many varieties of cacti. Try not to mix desert cacti with rainforest cacti, as the latter need more water and a slightly different soil to the desert varieties. The rainforest varieties are often trailing in nature and are perhaps best gifted in a hanging basket.

The Alpine Garden

Again, choose a shallow terracotta bowl, or similar, with good drainage, for your alpine display, which will be filled with cuttings that you have rooted from your own indoor display or outdoor rockery. Put a layer of stones in the bottom and then fill with a fine rich compost mixed with an equal proportion of horticultural grit.

Unlike cacti, alpines grow quite quickly, so leave a good space between each plant. Trailing plants should be planted at the edge of the container. Create a good mix of flowering alpines and succulents, for interest, and bear in mind that you are, in effect, creating a mini rockery, so the addition of some large stones or a piece of driftwood adds levels and texture. When choosing plants to put in an indoor garden, bear in mind that some alpines prefer an acid soil. Try not to mix them with plants that are happiest in a neutral soil, as they will not thrive. Water the plants in and finish off with a layer of gravel. Instruct the recipient to display the alpine garden by a sunny window and only water when the soil feels dry.

SUGGESTED PLANTS

Thrift ~ pink flowers in the summer
Sedum ~ mounds of evergreen purple foliage with yellow flowers in summer
Saxifrage ~ gorgeous rosettes of bright green with little pink star-shaped flowers.
Sempervivum ~ green and purple edged multi-layered star plants.
Thyme ~ low growing with dainty leaves that range from silver to dark green
Speedwell ~ pretty blue flowers in summer, but beware it spreads rapidly.

A Terrarium

Whereas miniature cacti and alpine gardens like to be open and dryish – terrariums (sometimes called bottle gardens) need to be humid. Nowadays there is such a wide selection of glass containers for terrariums, in all sorts of shapes and sizes, from clear to coloured glass. The containers can be closed, with a lid, or have an opening at the front or top. The closed type requires less maintenance because the plants create their own eco-system and recycle the moisture they create. They need a little water, maybe once a month, and some fresh air once a week (take the lid off for a day).

To create a terrarium, using plants that you already have in your own garden/s, make sure, first of all, that they are completely free of bugs or diseases. A terrarium can act like an incubator for such things and you will find that it will affect all the plants very quickly.

Put a layer of pebbles or pea gravel in the bottom of the container. Then put a layer of activated charcoal of about 1inch (2.5cms) thickness. Over that, put a layer of sphagnum moss, then cover that with about 2 inches (5cms) of compost.

The delicate work of planting up will begin. You may find various tools useful, like long-handled tweezers (often described as terrarium or plant tweezers), long handled barbeque implements and spoons (often described as latte or sundae spoons). Don't over fill the container. Don't plant the rootball of a plant right next to the glass. Fill in the spaces between the plants with sphagnum moss, coloured pebbles or sand. Pieces of wood or bark are not recommended as the constant damp may make them rot or grow mould. You can add interesting rocks.

Advise the recipient about care (see above) and to remove any excess moisture if the terrarium begins to mist up, by swabbing the interior glass with cotton wool. Terrariums should not be placed in direct sunlight. They need some shade and to keep relatively cool. (So not near any heat source, please – like a radiator)

SUGGESTED PLANTS

Pileas (like the Friendship plant) • Fittonias (like the Nerve plant) • Lichens
Ferns (like a Boston or Maidenhair fern) • Peperomia (like Money plants) • Spider plant
Ivy (miniature English ivy) • Polka Dot plant • Baby's Tears • Miniature Orchids

Making Gifts from Wood

Don't forget, when you come to making gifts from everything that grows in your garden, that trees can provide material for some exceptional crafts. However, remember that most wood needs a period of drying out, so, if you prune branches from your trees in late winter/early spring (which is the best time because wounds heal faster), then you will need the branches to spend all spring and summer drying out. Store them in a relatively dry place (out in the sun, if you have a warm summer) but don't bake them in very hot sun or they may crack.

Making a Bee House

There are over 240 species of wild bee in the UK that are called 'solitary bees' because they do not live in crowded hives with other bees. Making a bee house for yourself or an avid gardener/wildlife lover is an excellent way to use up any sizeable logs that may be created from pruning the trees in yours or your neighbour's gardens. Use only natural wood, not wood on sale in DIY or Garden Centres, which may have been treated with chemicals and may harm the bees and other insects.

Take a log of up to 6 inches (15cms) deep and drill a variety of holes in it. Do not drill all the way through the log. Drilling in to about a depth of 4inches (12cms) is sufficient. Make the holes varying widths (between ¼ to ½ inch diameter (5 to 10mm)). Make sure the 'tunnels' are smooth by using a round file of the appropriate diameter inside the holes. Sand the outside of the face of the log to make it smooth. Place the finished Bee House at about head height (hang from a tree perhaps?) and the holes facing south to get the most of any sun.

Wooden Jewellery

Little discs of wood make lovely brooches and pendants when painted, embellished and varnished. Brooch backings are easily glued on the finished disc or drill a hole and add a chain, leather strip or rope. Embellish the painted discs with pressed flowers or foliage and you have a very simple, attractive and unique gift.

Decorations from discs

A nice branch of about 4 ins (10cms) in diameter, can be sawn into lovely discs of about ½ inch (1cm) thickness. Then drill a hole in the top, to take ribbon or string.

These discs lend themselves especially to Christmas decorations. The warmth of the wood colour matches so well with winter foliage. Use a mixture of pressed or glycerine preserved leaves, tiny cones, acorns and beads. If you use real berries, acorns or rosehips they will have to be sprayed with several coats of varnish to seal and preserve them. It is also worth sealing the wood discs with coats of spray varnish before embellishing them. This prevents the wood from attracting any moisture when on display and stops the danger of mould. Use a strong glue, which dries clear, to attach the plant matter.

These wooden discs, cut from branches, if left plain and varnished, make excellent drinks coasters. You could, if you wished, before varnishing, paint designs on them or stick pretty paper on them. The surfaces need to be smooth and even in order to be used as drinks coasters, so even sticking pressed flowers on them would not really work.

Using Branches and Twigs

Many people like to have a vaseful of twigs on display during the autumn and winter – especially striking varieties such as the red dogwood branches, corkscrew hazel, curly willow or pussy willow. But sometimes, a sturdy branch can be used for other decorative purposes. Covering a branch with battery operated lights is an excellent addition to a dark corner of a room or to display in a window at night. Secure the branch in a container filled with readymade cement and allow to harden.

Then decorate the container, if you wish and put dark brown felt over the top of the set cement (to resemble soil). Then add your lights. Stand back and admire. Or you could decorate the branches with paper butterflies, fabric hearts or dried flowers.

Another excellent use for a branch with lots of side branches and twigs is as a jewellery stand. Paint the branch with silver or gold paint, if you wish, then set in a container (painted to match perhaps?) of cement as described above. Perfect for a teenager's display of necklaces, bracelets, bangles and rings.

Making use of Logs

If you are not going to use them to make bee houses, then use them as bases for decorative displays and table decorations. For example, you could drill a hole in the centre of a log, or pile of wooden discs, and insert a length of dowelling, that sticks above the log by about 3 inches (8cms). On the top of the dowelling, you could add a polystyrene ball, which you could cover with dried flower heads (see picture).

Alternatively, you could hollow out the centre of a log, big enough to take a medium sized flowerpot. If it is to go outside, then drill some drainage holes through. For inside the house, then line with plastic.

Yet another use is to hollow out a log and also drill some holes in as well, in random places along the top surface. Then you can slot in some of your dried flowers.

Dyes from your Plants

Dyeing yarns with plants is actually quite easy (if a little messy!) and will give you some stunning colours. If you have friends who knit or crochet, then you could gift them some unusual coloured yarn by dyeing natural coloured or white cotton or wool yarn (it must be made from natural fibres) using common plants from your garden. But warn your friends, when you present them with some naturally dyed yarn, that you cannot guarantee replicating the exact shade, should they want some more!

How to Dye

First, unravel all the yarn you intend to dye, put it in a clean bucket with some detergent for delicates and wash it thoroughly. This is to remove any chemical 'finishes' that have been added to the yarn in processing. Once you have washed and rinsed it, leave it wet. You will now need to prepare it for dyeing with a mordant (or fixative). You can buy alum powder online, or you can use soda crystals, salt, or bicarbonate of soda – easily purchased in your local supermarket. There are many other mordants that can be used. Each will subtly alter the colour of the plant dye, but the four mentioned above are the simplest to source.

So, three quarters fill a large stainless steel or enamel pan with water – neither of these will stain – put a dessertspoonful of your chosen mordant in the water and bring to the boil. Then add the yarn, turn the heat down slightly, and let the water and yarn simmer/rolling boil for about an hour. Turn off the heat and leave the pan and its contents to cool for twenty four hours. The yarn is now prepared (mordanted) for dyeing.

Empty the pan and refill with fresh water up to three quarters full again. This time, add your dye plants, tied up in a square of muslin or net curtain or a pop sock. (Please note that you will need the same weight of dye material as you have in yarn.) Boil for about an hour to fully release the dye from the plant matter. Then add the yarn, leaving the bag of plant matter in place. Boil cotton yarn for about an hour, stirring occasionally to distribute the dye evenly. Use a lower heat for wool, silk, alpaca, angora or cashmere yarn – a gentle simmer will do. Again, stir occasionally to distribute any dye still emanating from the plant matter. If you want a darker shade you can add an extra teaspoon of your mordant. Don't forget that the yarn colour will be slightly paler when dry.

Let the pan and its contents cool, then lift out the yarn and rinse it several times in clean water, before hanging it up to dry. Once dry, you can rewind it into skeins or balls for knitting or crocheting and present your gift with a handmade label proudly proclaiming that it is hand dyed using plants from your garden.

PLANTS AND THE COLOURS THEY WILL PRODUCE
*(Please note that all dyes will fade slightly with washing but any plants marked with * will create dyes that fade quickly with every wash)*

Acorns	Brown shades.
Beetroots*(not pickled)	Reddish brown.
Beetroots*(pickled)	Deep pink.
Blackberries	Gun metal grey.
Blueberries	Purplish blue.
Camellias	Pink shades depending upon the flower colour.
Dahlia	From pale yellow to a bright orange.
Daffodil	A yellow tinged with green.
Echinacea (purple)	Purple shades.
Elderberries	Purple shades.
Fennel	Brown shades.
Hibiscus	Purple shades.
Hollyhocks (dark red or purple)	Purple and maroon colours.
Lavender	Pink to pale lilac depending upon the colour of flowers.
Leafy greens (Spinach, lettuce etc.)	Various shades of green.
Marigolds	Depending upon the colour of the flowers, they will produce a yellow dye ranging from pale lemon to bright sunshine yellow.
Onion skins (yellow)	From a strong yellow, through the orange tones.
Onion skins (red)	Deep red. (Note: if you want a lighter red, mix yellow and red skins)
Red cabbage*	Purplish red.
Roses	Pink shades (even deep red roses only produce pink)

Christmas

This is the time of year when you can really use all of the wonderful things you have grown and preserved from your garden! If you have read the other books in this series, then you will have made, during the summer and autumn, edible gifts and health/beauty items and now, you can add homemade cards, wrappings, gifts boxes and decorations to your skills. You will impress your friends and family, save yourself a fortune and given all your efforts in the garden the true credit that they deserve. The following pages should give you some useful and simple ideas on how to make the most of everything your garden has offered up during the year.

Cards

Whether you have a garden, a balcony, or even a few pots indoors, I am willing to bet that, during the year, you have taken some photographs of your favourite plants. If these photographs happen to be seasonal – like your garden in the snow, or a beautiful poinsettia plant or Christmas cactus – then you have the perfect Christmas card. It doesn't matter if it isn't seasonal. Most people love a picture of a beautiful flower or of wildlife in the garden.

If you send out a lot of cards, then it is worth having a certain amount printed by one of the many 'instant', and cheap, printers around. Shown here are examples of cards that I had made from photos in my garden. Make sure that you put, inside the card, an explanation of the picture. For example – *My garden in the snow, 2012* or *Crocuses pushing through the snow in our garden, 2012*. Of course, you will note, when you go on the various printer's websites, that they can put your photos on many objects – mugs, hats, notebooks, notelets etc. Try not to be tempted!

If you only send out a few cards each year, then you could try printing them yourself, on your computer printer, using the best quality glossy paper or thin card and the highest quality print setting.

The other option for cards, which has been discussed elsewhere in this book (See page 74) is to decorate card blanks with pressed flowers. However, it is probably best if these are hand-delivered cards – unless you put them in very stiff cardboard envelopes – as the postal system is a little too arduous for delicate pressed flower pictures to survive, even though you should, ideally, finish off your creation with a covering of clear sticky backed plastic.

Wrapping Paper and Embellishments

It's nice to add some of your preserved plants as embellishments to plain wrapping paper, or gift bags and boxes. Look at the examples shown here. Glue them, for example to the lid of a gift box and it may end up as a keepsake on someone's dressing table. Make sure that all the plants, once glued in place and dry, have a coating, or two, of acrylic spray to help them withstand the dry warmth of central heating as they sit under the Christmas tree.

(NOTE: Don't put berries or beads on any gifts that are going to a house with small children or pets.)

The other alternative is to create your own wrapping paper. You can make some striking patterns by painting leaves different colours and pressing them on to large sheets of paper to make patterns.

Or, for smaller gifts, you could scatter the dried and pressed petals and leaves over a sheet of A4 paper which is covered in a coat of glue. Then use your computer's photocopying facility to copy the paper, once the glue is dry and you can lay it on the scanner bed. The result will be a very pretty and original piece of paper for wrapping small gifts.

Finally, you can , of course, gather together some of your lovely garden/plant photos and either print them out and glue them on to a large sheet of paper, or arrange them on to an A4 sheet on screen and print it out to wrap a small gift.

Table Decorations

This is where some of the wooden discs from your pruned tree branches (see page 84) come in useful, as bases for more elaborate decorations.

You can make some stunning small Christmas trees, using more material from your garden, such as fir cones, nuts, acorns, dried flower buds etc. You could paint some gold or leave them all natural.

HOW TO MAKE A TABLE TREE
You will need:

1 wooden disc for a base (Ideally you would want one that is at least 4ins diameter (10cms).

1 Styrofoam/Oasis cone with a base that is the same, or slightly, less than the diameter of the base disc. (A standard size, for example, is 4ins base diameter by 12ins high (10cms x 30cms))
A collection of small fir cones, nuts, little baubles, dried flower buds etc. Anything you wish to use.

A roll of fine florist/jewellery wire.

PVA glue

1. First, glue the base of the Oasis/polystyrene cone to the wooden disc and leave to dry until firm and immovable.
2. Put wire around the base layer of the small fir cones, leaving a short 'stalk' to push into the cone. Do the same with any flowers/foliage/baubles you are using. Glue some of the smaller nuts/berries/beads to the side of some of the wired fir cones and leave until they are firmly attached.
3. Working from the base upwards, push a layer of wired fir cones into the base of the Oasis/polystyrene cone, then, on the next layer, start adding more interesting combinations/colours and objects. Continue until you reach the top. Very simple!

MAKING A SMALL CANDLE WREATH

Again, using your wooden disc as a base, you will need a small shot glass or similar; a candle or tealight that fits into the shot glass; some foliage, fir cones, nuts and little baubles; some lace/ribbon/sequins to decorate the shot glass (optional).

Simply glue the base of the shot glass wherever you wish on the wooden disc. Then you can, if you wish, decorate the glass with lace, washi tape, sequins etc. It is easier to do that once the glass is glued down. Do not decorate near the rim of the glass or put anything flammable around the rim. If you want to paint designs on the glass, you will have to do that before it is glued down. Pop the candle into the glass and start to glue to the base the decorative pieces that you want to place around the glass.

AN ALTERNATIVE

Finally, a lovely idea for a fake Christmas Terrarium. If you have an empty goldfish bowl or glass fruit bowl, you can make a lovely centrepiece for your table. Buy some very cheap artificial snow (you can buy it online – either white or with some glitter in it), put a generous layer in the bottom of your bowl, then add fir cones, small pieces of branches, dried flowers, painted nuts or pebbles – anything that you find attractive! Don't put a candle in there, as it could be a fire risk, but you could add battery operated fairy lights if you wish.

Decorations from Branches and Twigs

We all know someone who lives in a small flat and has no floor space for a Christmas tree. So, you could gift them a wall hanging tree instead! It's a very simple construction of branches, graduated in size. You could either drill holes in either end of each branch and tie a large knot in the rope above and below each branch, as you pass the rope through, or simply tie the rope around each branch, leaving enough rope to create a hanging loop. The branches could be left as natural branches (but perhaps varnished to preserve them and prevent bark splitting off when stored), or they could be painted a fashionable or Christmassy colour. Then just add decorations to hang from each branch. These could be natural too (gold sprayed pine cones, for example).

Or you could just spray a lovely bundle of twigs with a sparkly spray paint and arrange them in a pot filled with ready made craft cement. A friend of mine just sticks them in the plastic tub of cement/plaster and leaves it to harden, then decorates the plastic pot! She also puts some sphagnum moss over the hardened cement to cover it up. Decorate the twigs with baubles and you have a lovely Christmas display for a mantelpiece or cupboard.

Or, if your recipient doesn't have anywhere to store Christmas decorations, for use the next year, then an alternative is to gift three decorated branches from a fir tree, attach to the wall with a removable, tough adhesive tape (see picture). Then they can be taken down after Christmas and recycled.

Single branches (with or without foliage) are an attractive way of displaying homemade decorations in small rooms.

If you are lucky enough to have a willow tree in your garden, or have grown some tall grasses that take well to being hung upside down to dry or stood in a vase with desiccant, like pampas, meadow, the quaintly named quaking grass and Job's Tears, then you can use these to create all manner of wreaths, stars, hearts and other shapes for Christmas décor. Green willow (which has just been cut and is flexible) stripped of its bark, can be plaited into wreaths, and other garden items such as cones, nuts and berries can be added. Grasses can be dyed or painted different colours and bundled together to form wreaths or other shapes (like the red star in the picture). Grasses have to be tied together to keep a shape and you can do this by either using other pieces of grass, so that they blend in, or using colourful ribbons or lace to be eye catching. All these decorations will benefit from a spray coating of varnish, once assembled, to preserve them for use in future years.

Scented Gifts

Using the perfume of your plants as gifts is a wonderful idea and the simplest way of doing that is to either gift some pot pourri (see page 7) or to fill some attractive, easily sewn, bags or dolls with dried, scented petals. Lavender bags are easy to make and designed to hang in wardrobes to not only make clothes smell wonderful but also to keep moths and flies at bay (they hate the smell of lavender!).

HOW TO MAKE A LAVENDER BAG

You will need:

- 2 x 6inch (15cms) square thin cotton
- 2 x 6inch long (15cms) lace
- 1 x 12inch (30cms) lace or ribbon
- 1 x 24inch x ¼inch (60cms x 0.5cms) ribbon
- 1 x 8inch x ¼inch (20cms x 0.5cms) ribbon
- Dried lavender

Diagram 1 — *Sew around three edges*, *Lace*, *Right side of fabric*

1. This bag will have French seams, so that it will last for a long time and can be refilled again and again. So, take your two square pieces of cotton and put the wrong sides together. Lay the pieces of lace across the middle of the right sides of the fabric, in the same place on both pieces. Pin in place, then sew along three sides ¼inch (0.5cms) from the edge *(See Diagram 1)*.

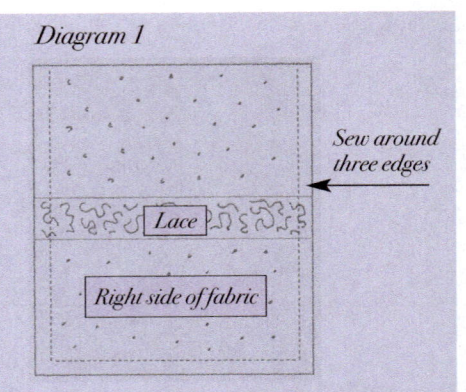

2. Turn inside out and repeat, stitching ¼inch (0.5cms) in from the same three edges. Then turn right side out again. You have now enclosed the edges in a French seam to avoid the cotton fraying.

3. Now bind around the open edge of the bag, with lace or cotton *(see Diagram 2)*.

4. Take the two pieces of ¼inch (0.5cms) ribbon. Find the centre of the 24inch (60cms) ribbon, make the 8inch (20cms) ribbon into a loop and sew it to the centre of the long ribbon *(see Diagram 3)*.

5. Sew the ribbon and loop combination to the middle of one side of the lavender bag. *(See Diagram 3)* about 1inch (2cms) from the top of the bag.

6. Fill with lavender and tie up firmly! It is now ready to hang in a wardrobe.

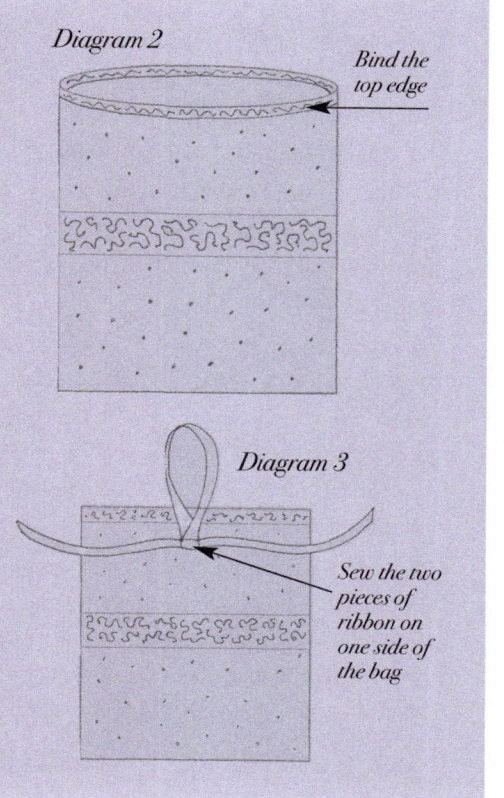

Diagram 2

Bind the top edge

Diagram 3

Sew the two pieces of ribbon on one side of the bag

HOW TO MAKE A SCENTED DOLLY

This is meant to sit on a dressing or bedside table and gently perfume the air.

You will need:

1 x 8 - 9inch (21-23cms) diameter circle of thin cotton (use a side/tea plate to draw around. They are roughly the right size)

1 x 4.5inch (12cms) diameter circle of matching thin cotton (use a CD or DVD to draw around).

Sufficient ½inch (1cm) wide lace to go around the edge of both circles.

1 x 1.5 inch (3cms) diameter wooden bead (any colour you wish or plain wood)

1 x basic wooden barbeque skewer or a long Cook's Match (with the head broken off)

Craft glue

Dried lavender or pot pourri

Uncooked white long grain rice

1. Sew lace around the outside edge of both fabric circles (on the right side of the fabric).
2. Put thick craft glue over 1.5inch (3cms) of the blunt end of the barbeque skewer or match and insert it into the hole of the wooden bead. Lay flat and leave to dry until firmly stuck.
3. If necessary, paint the wooden bead whatever colour you wish, white, tan, brown and leave to dry. You may need more than one coat. (Stick the skewer/match in a pencil pot or a piece of foam whilst you paint the bead and allow it to dry).
4. Sew, by hand, a long running stitch around the two circles, ¼inch (0.5cms) from the lace edge, leaving a long piece of cotton free, so that you can gently pull on both to gather them up *(See Diagram 1)*.
5. Partially gather the larger circle – don't tie off yet – leaving enough room to spoon measures of rice and lavender into the 'body' of the doll, until it is quite full, and the shape has rounded out. (The rice, in a 60/40 split with the flower heads, will absorb the lavender scent.) Now finish gathering the 'body' fabric until it is quite closed and, thread a needle with the pulled through thread, sew it firmly in place and cut off the excess.
6. Pull the gathering thread through on the small circle, until you have an opening the same size as the wooden bead 'head'. Sew it off and glue the 'mob cap' into place on the top of the bead. Leave to dry until it is firm.
7. Measure the length of the 'body' from base to 'lacy collar' and cut off the bamboo skewer below the head to the same measurement. Draw the 'face' on the 'head' with a black pen, then just insert the skewer into the 'body', where the rice will keep it upright. It is not necessary to sew the bamboo skewer into place. Just advise the recipient not to pick up the doll by its 'head'!

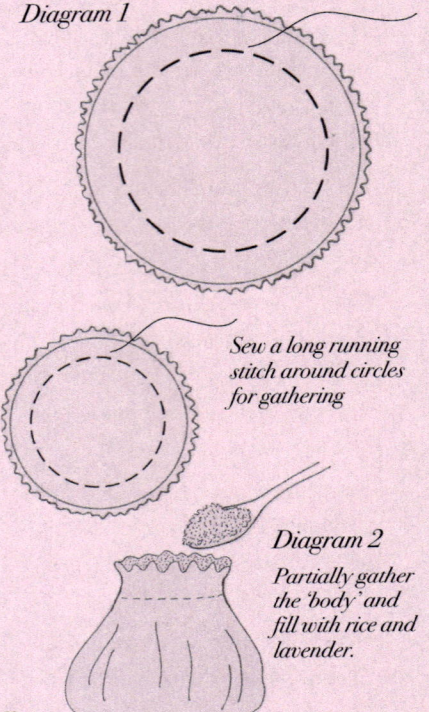

Diagram 1

Sew a long running stitch around circles for gathering

Diagram 2

Partially gather the 'body' and fill with rice and lavender.

SECTION 4 : *Treats*

This is a culinary section, of sorts, as it does cover food and drink but the emphasis is on special things such as cocktails, mocktails, ice creams, ice lollies, finger food and party snacks – the sort of things that you can contribute to a garden party or winter gathering. The bounty of your garden can be ever versatile and you can be endlessly creative with the items that you gift to any special gathering.

HERBS FOR COCKTAILS AND MOCKTAILS

Often, the simple addition of a herb, or herb combinations, can elevate a drink from merely refreshing to a taste sensation. Often, the best way to do this is to freeze herbs, aromatic plant leaves and flowers when they are at peak perfection. You can freeze them in ice cube trays using plain water or some of the diluted cordials that you have made (see page 4), depending upon what drinks you are planning to create later. Always use herbs and plants that have not been sprayed with pesticides or grown near a busy road.

Here are some suggested combinations:

Herb/plant	Frozen in:	Goes with:
Sweet basil	Water or strawberry/raspberry cordial	Strawberry or raspberry based cocktail
Mint	Water or apple cordial/juice	Apple or lime-based drinks
Lemon thyme Lemon balm	Water	Lemon-based drinks
Sweet cicely Lemon balm Lemon thyme Angelica stem	Elderflower cordial	Any fruit-based cocktail
Lemon verbena Mint Rosemary Scented rose petals	Elderflower cordial	Lemonade bases

Herb/plant	Frozen in:	Goes with:
Snippets of elderflowers		
Scented rose petals		
Sprigs of lavender	Rosehip or raspberry cordial	Any drink
Pineapple sage		
Lemon balm	Elderflower cordial	Any tropical fruit base
Rosemary	Rhubarb cordial	Any lemon-based drink
Sprigs of lavender	Blueberry cordial	Any dark berry drink.

Using Edible Flowers in Drinks

Edible flowers can be either frozen in water to provide decoration, fragrance and added flavour to drinks, or they can be dried and sprinkled across the top of a drink. (See page 66 for plant drying techniques). Dried flowers look particularly spectacular floating on a milk/yoghurt-based cocktail, drink or smoothie.

A tot of floral syrup can be added to the drink, for extra flavour. (See page 13).

Again, these should be flowers free from any toxic sprays, pesticides etc. and not grown near a busy road.

Wash gently before freezing. Use silicon ice cube trays with lids, to stop the flowers bouncing up out of the water.

For a list of edible flowers, see next page.

Flower	What to pick	Commonly used in:
Borage	small whole flower. No stem	Pimm's cocktails
Chamomile	whole single flower. No stem	Non-alcoholic drinks, tisanes
Dahlia	small whole flower. No stem	Cocktails
Daisy	small whole flower. No stem	Lemonades
Hibiscus	small whole flower. No stem	Sparkling wines
Lavender	whole small fresh sprigs	Cocktails
Lilac	whole small fresh sprigs or petals	Cordials
Marigold	small whole flower. No stem	Cocktails
Nasturtium	small whole flower and petals	Cordials
Pansy	small whole flower. No stem	All cold drinks
Rose (scented)	small whole flower, buds, petals	Sparkling wines
Viola	small whole flower. No stem	All cold drinks

What Else can you Bring to the Party?

Firm berries freeze very well in ice cube trays. Blueberries, red, black and white currants, firm raspberries, firm blackberries, tayberries, loganberries, lingonberries, josta berries – the list is almost endless! Strawberries do not freeze well, however, and are best brought to the table fresh and sliced into drinks.

If you are fortunate enough to live in an area where you can grow citrus fruits in your garden, then those can be contributed frozen or fresh, sliced or squeezed into drinks.

Fresh, homemade tomato juice, freshly picked celery, and the necessary herbs, can all be brought along to create Bloody Mary's – either alcoholic or non-alcoholic. Freshly sliced cucumber can be used in so many drinks, and also as a decoration.

Small cocktail onions go well in dry martinis. Frozen grapes are great in drinks, but don't bother to freeze them in water, as with smaller berries. Just freeze them as they are, on trays, then bag them up and keep them in the freezer for when you need them.

As for treats that can be eaten, whilst drinking that cocktail/mocktail – well just look at the following pages for some very tasty ideas.

A Berry Good Idea

The greatest way to add instant colour and powerful flavour to drinks is by using berry powder. Drying your own berries is very simple and the resulting powders can be stored in clean dry jars in a cool area, to be used whenever you want. Berry powder can also be used to colour and flavour anything – like, porridge, yoghurt, smoothies, custards, jellies and mousses. An all-round versatile hit of garden superfood in a handy container!

If you are a large-scale gardener, then you may possibly have a dehydrator. In which case, creating berry powder is easy-peasy.

Most people won't have a dehydrator and therefore need to dry out berries and other fruit in the oven. Take the stones out of cherries and halve them, similarly sloes or any other stoned fruit. Grapes need the seeds removed. Strawberries should be sliced. If you have big fat blueberries or large blackberries, then they will need to be cut in half. You are aiming to make everything on the baking tray a similar size, so that they will dehydrate in the oven at the same speed.

If you want to be efficient and carefully fill your jars with powder from just one type of berry/fruit, then you will need to separate the fruits and dehydrate them in batches.

Spread the fruit out, in a single layer with spaces between each fruit piece, on a sheet of baking paper on an oven tray and bake at a low temperature (135F or 60C or Gas Mark ¼) for at least 8 hours (overnight is not a good idea, as you really need to keep checking on them every now and then. Obviously, a special dehydrator unit can be utilised overnight. In fact, most dehydrators take at least 1½ to 2 days to process several shelves of fruit).

Let the berries/fruit cool and then blend them into a powder in a blender or food processor. Store and label. One teaspoon should be enough to add flavour and colour to anything.

Candies!

Sorry folks, but this means sugar and spoiling the young ones with special treats. As long as it's only now and then, eh? And, of course, as it is the produce of your garden and made by hand, there will be no nasty additives.

FUDGE APPLES

Better than traditional toffee apples because the coating is chewy rather than brittle.

The trick to keeping the fudge on the apple, when you coat it is, firstly, that the apple has come from your garden and won't have a coat of wax on it, like supermarket apples. Secondly, you need to dunk the apples in boiling water for one minute, to make the skin slightly softer and, finally, using a serrated knife, gently score the apples all over with a light criss-cross pattern.

Ingredients

6 small eating apples, remove the stalks but that is all • 3ozs (75g) golden syrup • 6ozs (150g) light brown soft sugar • 3ozs (75g) butter • 6ozs (150g) condensed milk (not evaporated – you want the thick stuff)

How to make:

1. Having put the apples in boiling water for one minute, allowed them to cool, and scored the skin, now push a thick lolly stick into each apple at the stalk end. You want to push it in halfway, so that it won't come out easily, (but don't push it right through and out the other end!)
2. Melt the syrup, sugar, butter and condensed milk in a heavy saucepan over a low heat. Use a long-handled wooden spoon to stir it frequently to make sure it doesn't stick or burn. Take care that the heat is not too high, otherwise the mixture will spit and you could end up with burns on your hand or arm!
3. It will take about 15 minutes to reach the right consistency. If you have a sugar

thermometer you want it to read 115C.

Otherwise, have a bowl of iced water to hand and, if you drop a small amount of the mixture into it and it forms a ball, then it is done.

4. Let the fudge cool a little (not too much or it will start to solidify), then take each apple by the stick and roll it around in the fudge until it is coated. Either put the fudge apples downwards on a tray covered in greaseproof paper, or push the stick end into a block of florist's foam. Either way, leave enough space between the apples for the air to circulate and cool them.

5. Whilst they are still a little warm and sticky, you can roll them in some additional coverings, like chopped nuts or hundreds and thousands. However, to add a layer or decoration of chocolate, it is best to wait until they are completely cold.

HEALTHY ROCKY ROAD

Easy peasy. If you are lucky enough to have a nut tree in your garden, plus your fruit harvest (some of which you have just candied – see page opposite) then this is the most popular treat for children and adults alike. You can even make it vegan by melting dairy free chocolate. Or melt white chocolate and add some drops of food colouring to make pink or green or even purple chocolate, if you want. Traditional Rocky Road has little marshmallows in it, which you can add, if you wish. But just using your own fruits and nuts will make it a bit healthier.

There is no point in giving you a list of ingredients because you will use your own judgement as to how much chocolate you need to melt and how many handfuls of fruits and nuts you need to add, depending upon how many treats you want to dispense!

You can also melt the chocolate in the microwave, to make life simpler.

Spread the melted choc, nut and fruit mixture out onto a baking sheet, lined with greaseproof paper. Put it in the fridge to set and then break it into pieces before piling it into a bowl.

It won't last long!

CANDIED FRUIT

You can glaze most types of fruit but it is best to not try to candy slices of fruit that contain a lot of water, like citrus fruits or melons (especially watermelons). Most berries, apples, pears, apricots, firm plums, greengages, damsons and strawberries work well. Overripe fruit will have too much juice in it. You can even candy strips of orange and lemon rind and carrots, to use as cake decorations.

Wash and remove any stones, stalks, cores and pips from the fruit and cut everything into bite-size pieces.

Ingredients

6ozs (150g) white sugar • 6ozs (150g) clear honey • 12 fl ozs (350ml) water

How to make:

1. Boil the sugar, honey and water over a moderate heat, using a long handled wooden spoon to stir it gently to stop any sticking or burning. I recommend wearing an oven mitten on the hand that does the stirring, as this mixture has to get up to 112C (235F) on a candy thermometer. Alternatively, when you drop a blob into iced water, it should form a thread of hardened syrup.
2. Lower a handful of fruit pieces into the syrup, using a slotted spoon. Then turn down the heat, so that the syrup just simmers the fruit until it looks translucent. (About 20 minutes).
3. Gently fish the fruit out, with the slotted spoon, and place them on a tray covered in greaseproof paper, to cool. Repeat with more fruit, until you have run out.
4. Once the candied fruit has cooled, you can pile it into a bowl, in which you have put 2 or 3 tablespoons of fine granulated sugar, (some people prefer icing sugar) and roll the fruit around until it is thoroughly coated.

Ice Creams, Sorbets and Lollies

Nothing says 'treat' like some form of icy comfort on a hot day and you don't need a fancy ice cream maker to create one. And, of course, you will have the fresh berry produce of your garden, or your stored berry powder (see page 102), jams (see page 11), cordials (see page 4) or fruit/flower syrups (see page 13) to add the flavour and colour.

BASIC ICE CREAM

This is for a creamy, smooth ice dessert base. The mascarpone, Greek yoghurt and milk can all be replaced with plant-based alternatives – but make sure the yoghurt is thick.

Ingredients

8ozs (200g sugar) * • 14ozs (350g) plain mascarpone cheese • 4ozs (100g) plain Greek yoghurt • 8fl.ozs (250ml) milk • 3fl.ozs (100ml) water

(* you can cut down on the sugar and water by removing 2 ozs of sugar and 1fl.oz water, if you are going to use fruit syrup or jam to flavour the ice cream. If you are going to use fresh fruit puree, then leave the quantities as they are.)

How to make:

1. If using fresh fruit to flavour the ice cream, then wash and puree about 8ozs (200g) of your chosen fruit and set aside.
2. Make a sugar syrup with the sugar and water, stirring all the time, until it boils. Then turn the heat down and simmer it for about three minutes until it is a little thicker and clings to the spoon a little. If you are using your own fruit syrup or cordial to flavour, then add 3 tablespoons of that to the syrup mixture.

3. Beat together the mascarpone, yoghurt and milk and add the sugar syrup, blending it in well. Then, if you are using fresh fruit puree, blend that into the mixture. Taste it and, if you feel that it needs more flavour, then add some berry powder (see page 102) or another spoonful of cordial.

4. Place in a freezer container and freeze. You will have to remove it from the freezer every hour, for about six hours and stir it thoroughly to make sure that ice crystals don't form.

5. Allow to defrost slightly before serving. Add extra whole berries to garnish the dish. Maybe drizzle over a little fruit syrup. Perhaps a sprig of lemon balm or mint.

ICE LOLLIES

Oh. So. Easy. Basically, blend a smoothie with fresh fruit, plain yoghurt and a little sugar. Again, substituting dairy for plant-based can make a vegan lolly.

Ingredients *(makes about 4 medium sized lollies)*

6ozs (150g) raw washed, stoned, cut up fruit, or sieved fruit (in the case of any berries with pips/seeds) • 5ozs (125/130g) thick Greek yoghurt • 2 tablespoons of white sugar

How to make:

1. Blitz in a food processor or blender, pour into lolly moulds, add sticks, and freeze. That's it!

BASIC SORBET

Sorbets are also easy to make (although you still have to mash them up every so often, if you don't have an ice-cream maker, until you get an ice crystal-free mix). And sorbets, of course, are definitely vegan! This recipe is only for fresh fruit. Make sure that all pips/stones are removed either before cooking, or afterwards, by sieving. Nothing worse than lots of raspberry pips in a mouthful of sorbet! You will need about 2lbs (900g) of fresh fruit but if you feel that the flavour is not intense enough, then spoonfuls of cordial or fruit syrup could be added. Sometimes, we gardeners get years where our strawberries or raspberries are not as flavourful as they should be, due to circumstances beyond our control!

Ingredients

6ozs (150g) white sugar • 4fl.ozs (120ml) water • 2lbs (900g) fresh fruit • 1 tablespoon of lemon juice

How to make:

1. Wash, (stone and cut up, if need be) and puree fruit (sieve if required), retaining all pulp and juice (discarding any skins and pips).
2. Make the sugar syrup with the sugar and water in a saucepan over a high heat, stirring all the time (use a wooden spoon) and boiling for one minute.
3. Let the syrup cool slightly and then combine with the fruit puree and the tablespoon of lemon juice. Test for taste and supplement with fruit syrup, berry powder or cordial, if necessary.
4. Put in a freezer container and allow to set but remove after two hours to mash it up again. Return to the freezer. You may have to do this a couple more times (every two hours) to get the right consistency.
5. Serve with the appropriate decorations.

GRANITA OR SLUSH

This very popular Sicilian dessert/treat (which is basically flavoured ice in a glass) can be achieved in three ways:

1. Only mash up a sorbet mixture once, so that the end result has lots of ice crystals in it and has a very grainy texture.
2. Make fruity ice cubes and then smash them up in a plastic bag to create smaller pieces of flavoured ice to go into a glass.
3. Make plain ice cubes, smash them up, put them in a glass and pour fruit syrup over them.

EXCITING COMBINATIONS FOR BOOZY GRANITAS *(Adults only!)*

Mix everything up well, making sure the sugar is dissolved, before pouring it over. You could use a spoonful of agave syrup instead, if preferred.

1. Half a glass of apple juice, 1 shot of Aperol and a teaspoon of sugar.
2. Lime juice (from one lime), strawberries (mashed up), 1 shot of tequila, 1 teaspoon sugar
3. Half a glass of rosé wine, two teaspoons of floral syrup (preferably rose), half a teaspoon of vanilla essence.

Stuffed, Fried and Dipped!

Certain flowers, if large enough, can be stuffed and fried easily and many fruits can be deliciously stuffed and baked.

Perhaps the most common flower to be stuffed is the courgette (zucchini) flower but you can easily use the same recipe for large nasturtium and hibiscus, pumpkin and squash flowers.

STUFFED FLOWERS *(8 savoury pieces)*

8 large courgette/zucchini flowers • Oil for deep frying

Ingredients *(for the batter)*

1 large egg • 4ozs (100g) plain flour • Large pinch of bicarbonate of soda • 5fl.ozs (160ml/¾cup/10tbspns) very cold sparkling water

For the filling:

8ozs (200g) tub chive and herb cottage cheese • 6ozs (150g) soft goat's cheese (could be peppered) • Zest of 1 lemon • 2 teaspoons of paprika • Generous sprinkle of dried (not fresh) thyme • A few leaves of chopped fresh basil

How to make:

1. Make the batter by whisking the flour, bicarbonate of soda and the egg together until smooth and free from any lumps.
2. Gradually add the fizzy water until you have a batter the consistency of cream.
3. In another bowl, beat together the cheeses, lemon zest and herbs/spices until you are satisfied that all the flavours are well mixed together.
4. Wash the flowers gently and leave to dry on kitchen paper. Once dry, carefully remove the stamen from the middle of each flower, then spoon in to the flower a couple of spoonfuls of the filling. Twist the end of the petals together to make a parcel.
5. Make sure that your frying oil is hot enough, then dip the stuffed flowers into the batter and gently add to the oil. Fry for a couple of minutes, turning gently with a slotted spoon.
6. Lift out on to kitchen paper to absorb the oil.
7. Delicious warm or cold.

NO COOK STUFFED FRUIT

Large strawberries are excellent for this. Using a thin, sharp knife, slice the tops off the strawberries and hollow out a little of the fruit inside. Using a piping bag, you can then pipe inside plain cream, flavoured cream, melted chocolate, chocolate spread – your choice! Then pop the tops back on.

STUFFED AND BAKED FRUIT

Such an easy recipe and can be used for peaches, nectarines, large plums and apricots. Alcohol can be added as well!

RECIPE *(For 4 peaches or nectarines or 8 plums or apricots)*

Ingredients

Your chosen frui t • 4ozs (100g) of crushed amaretti biscuits • 2ozs (50g) finely diced dried mixed peel • 1ozs (25g/2.5 tablespoons) light brown sugar • 1 tablespoon of almond essence • 1ozs (25g) butter • 1 cup (250ml) sweet white wine or, if no alcohol is preferred, white grape juice.

How to make:

1. Wash and halve the fruit, removing the stone and slightly hollowing out the stone cavity (but not by much).
2. Mix together, vigorously, the fruit pulp, dried mixed peel, crushed amaretti biscuits, almond essence and half of the white wine.
3. Spoon the mixture into the centre of the fruit half, making a small dome in each.
4. Put a sliver of butter on the top of each dome. Then sprinkle each stuffed fruit with brown sugar and the remaining wine or juice.
5. Cook for about 35 minutes in an oven temperature of 180C (350F Gas Mark 4) until the peaches are soft and the filling is golden brown. (Do not allow to burn)
6. Serve cold as finger food or warm with cream.

Flower and Fruit Fritters

ELDERFLOWERS

The flower heads of the elder tree are very popular as a sweet and aromatic treat and so easy to make.

Ingredients

10-15 elderflower heads • 4ozs (100g) self-raising flour • 2 tsp cornflour • 1 large egg
5fl oz (150ml) sparkling water • 2 tsp white sugar • Pinch of salt • 1 tsp vanilla essence
Oil for frying • Icing sugar to dust over the fritters

How to make:

1. Wash flowerheads and lay them carefully on a tea towel or kitchen paper to dry.
2. Whisk together the flour, egg, cornflour, salt, and vanilla essence. When all is smooth, then add the sparkling water gradually.
3. Dip one flowerhead at a time in the batter and then fry for no more than one minute each.
4. Remove and put on kitchen paper to soak up any excess oil.
5. Serve as soon as possible, dusting with icing sugar first.

FRUIT FRITTERS

Any fruit can be done in this way – but the most popular are apples (peeled, cored and cut into thick rings, pears (peeled, cut into halves or quarters and the core removed), plums and apricots (don't peel but cut in half and remove the stones).

Ingredients

You want a slightly thicker batter for this, so:
3 medium sized apples/ pears or 12 plums/apricots • 6ozs (150g) plain flour • 2 large eggs
4 flat teaspoons of white sugar • 2 teaspoons baking powder • Large pinch of salt • 5 fl ozs (160ml) milk or plant milk • 1 tablespoon vegetable oil • A small bowl of white sugar with cinnamon added (for coating after cooking) • Oil for frying

How to make:

1. Wash and prepare the fruit as suggested above.
2. Stir all the dry ingredients together (except the cinnamon sugar).
3. Add the beaten eggs, milk and vegetable oil.
4. Dip a few fruit pieces into the batter and then lower them into the hot frying oil. Fry them for 4-5 minutes, turning them with a slotted spoon. When golden, lift the fruit out and place on kitchen paper to drain. Continue to dip the fruit pieces in batter and then fry and drain.
5. Once they are done and still warm, coat the fruit fritters in cinnamon sugar and place on a serving plate.

DIPPED FRUIT

Everyone loves a chocolate fondue and the joy of dipping fruit pieces into dark, milk, white or caramel chocolate, butterscotch sauce or a sweet custard.

However, if the party is not in your house or garden, and the hosts don't want the mess of a fondue, then you can pre-dip fruit in any of the chocolate options, and also butterscotch, if you have a recipe that sets quite well. If you dip them in white chocolate, then you could sprinkle over some of your berry powders to add extra flavour.

Party Nibbles

VEGETABLE CRISPS

A drinks party is just not the same without savoury nibbles and this is where your garden produce can come in really handy. Crisps (chips) don't have to be just made of potato – no, no. Root vegetables make great crisps. All you need is a mandoline slicer (so that you can slice the veg into really fine slices) and some great seasoning.

Some of the more fibrous root vegetable slices (such as carrot, parsnip, swede, potato, sweet potato, celeriac and turnip) will need to be dropped into boiling water for two minutes (blanched), to break down the fibres, and then fished out and plunged into a bowl of cold water to stop the cooking process. (Don't blanch beetroot or courgette slices).

Then, you can cook them either by dehydration, or by frying.

Dehydration, in a low oven, should take about 4-5 hours, until the slices are crisp. Set your oven on its lowest possible setting, spread out the vegetable slices on a baking tray, lined with greaseproof paper, and keep checking on them every hour. Some slices will take longer to dehydrate, like beetroot and courgette, because they contain more water.

Frying is simple and very quick. If the fat is hot enough and the slices thin enough, they will fry very quickly, so don't take your eye off them! Have a large tray, covered in kitchen paper, to hand, so that you can scoop the slices out with a slotted spoon and put them to one side to drain off any excess oil.

If you have fried your crisps, then you can immediately sprinkle over your seasoning mix by putting them in a large bowl and turning them over and over with one hand, whilst sprinkling seasoning with the other.

If you have dehydrated the crisps, then you will need to lay them out on a tray first and lightly spray them with a fine mist of oil, sprinkle seasoning over, wait for five minutes, then turn over the crisps and repeat the process. If making salt and vinegar crisps then mist them over with a layer of vinegar first, wait for ten minutes, then mist over the oil and sprinkle the seasoning.

Suggested seasonings:

Spicy	Salt & vinegar	Paprika
Salt	Cider vinegar (in a spray bottle)	Salt
Pepper	Salt	Pepper
Chili flakes	Pepper	Dried smoked paprika
Powdered garlic		(or dried hot paprika)

KALE CRISPS

Easy to make in the oven and they taste like crispy seaweed. Try them with an exotic Middle-Eastern flavouring like Palestinian Za'atar, Lebanese Ras El Hanout (sometimes called Lebanese 7 Spice) or Turkish Pul Biber (grind up the flakes into a powder to sprinkle).

How to make:

Put the oven on a low setting – 150C (300F/Gas Mark 2). Remove the stalks from the kale and wash the medium-sized leaves. Dry the leaves and put in a large bowl. Spray a fine mist of oil, whilst turning over the leaves, to ensure an even distribution. Then sprinkle over your chosen seasoning, whilst turning over the leaves again, to ensure that every leaf gets some spice. Spread the leaves out on a baking tray covered in greaseproof paper. Bake for about 20 minutes until crisp. Leave to cool before serving.

POTATO, SWEET POTATO AND VEGETABLE FRIES

Another very simple option is to give people vegetable chips (fries) and dips. Some vegetables (like sweet potato) benefit from a quick fry, then drained for a rest, then another quick fry. It makes them crisper. Keep the cooked fries warm in a very, very low oven, whilst you are preparing the others, then you can whisk them out to your guests, after lightly seasoning them.

SPICY NUTS AND SEEDS

This topic (with recipes) has already been covered on pages 24 and 25. Definitely a must for any drinks party.

ROASTED SAVOURY BROAD BEANS

Ingredients

Podded broad beans – split into halves • Olive oil • Salt • Black pepper

(Optional other flavourings: paprika, chili oil, any dried herbs)

How to make:

1. Put the broad beans into a bowl and drizzle some olive oil or chili oil over the beans. Turn the beans over and over, gently, until they are coated with the oil.
2. Lay the beans out in a single layer on a baking tray and sprinkle salt, pepper and any herbs over them.
3. Roast in a preheated oven (180C/350C/Gas Mark 5) for about half an hour until they are crisp.

Cakes Made From Veg
(and no-one will know)

When you have a glut of certain vegetables, it is nice to be able to use them in all sorts of things, including cake treats. Grated vegetables give quite a lot of moisture to a cake and this is why they work so well. And the flavours/spices you add, make the vegetables almost invisible to the palate. Everyone knows and loves carrot cake but they probably will never have tried a cake made with beetroot, or with butternut squash. Just one basic recipe will serve and the added ingredients are listed opposite.

BASIC RECIPE

- 2 large eggs
- 4 fl.ozs (120 ml) vegetable oil
- 4ozs (100g) sugar
- 8ozs (200g) self-raising flour
- 1 teaspoon baking powder
- Pinch of salt

BASIC FROSTING

- 3ozs (75g) softened butter or spread
- 2 tablespoons of icing sugar
- 6ozs (150g) plain cream cheese
- ½ teaspoon vanilla essence

(* for the beetroot chocolate cake, add about 2ozs (50g) of cocoa powder)

How to make:

1. Preheat the oven to 180C (350F or Gas Mark 5).
2. Mix together the sugar, flour, salt and baking powder in a large bowl.
3. In a separate bowl, whisk together the eggs and the oil, then add it to the dry ingredients, whisking some more to a smooth batter.
4. Then add your special ingredients (see opposite).

FOR A PUMPKIN OR BUTTERNUT SQUASH GINGER CAKE, ADD:

- 8ozs (200g) uncooked, rind-removed and grated pumpkin or squash
- 1 large apple, peeled, cored and grated
- 2 teaspoons of ground ginger
- 2 globes of bottled stem ginger, finely chopped
- 2 teaspoons of the ginger syrup from the bottled stem ginger.

FOR A BEETROOT AND CHOCOLATE CAKE, ADD:

- 8ozs (200g) uncooked, peeled and grated beetroot
- 4ozs (100g) plump sultanas
- 3ozs (75g) cocoa powder

FOR A CARROT CAKE ADD:

- 8ozs (200g) uncooked, peeled and grated carrots
- 2ozs (50g) chopped nuts (optional)
- ½ teaspoon mixed spice
- ½ teaspoon cinnamon

Finally, bake your vegetable cake for about 1 hour, testing that it is firm before you remove it. Otherwise cover the top with tinfoil and leave it to bake for another 15 minutes.

Fruit Instead of Veg?

You can be desperate to use up a glut of fruit as well, of course. So, the basic recipe on page 118, still stands.

FOR AN APPLE CAKE, ADD:

- 2 large, peeled, cored and diced apples
- 1 teaspoon of cinnamon and 1 teaspoon of lemon essence.

FOR A BERRY CAKE, ADD:

- 6ozs (150g) of berries (cut them up if they are large). Blueberries, elderberries, blackberries and raspberries all cook well. (Put 2 teaspoons of berry powder or 2 teaspoons of undiluted berry cordial in the frosting.)

FOR A PEAR CAKE, ADD:

- 3 medium-sized pears, peeled, cored and diced
- 1 teaspoon of ground ginger and 1 teaspoon of mixed spice.

Strawberries do not cook well in cakes and cherries require a different basic cake recipe. Gooseberries are a bit too sharp. Use your gluts to make jams (Page 10) and then use those in sandwich cakes!

Jellies, Fools and Meringues

Individual pots of treats are always welcome at gatherings and they always look so pretty as well! Summer desserts don't just have to be for summer. If you freeze berries then you can use them all year round. Just make sure that they are nice firm berries that will retain their shape and flavour when they thaw. Strawberries don't work – they tend to go mushy after thawing. Gooseberries can often wrinkle after thawing and lose some of their colour. Firm raspberries, mulberries, blackberries, loganberries, tayberries, blueberries, all the currants and stoned cherries will freeze well. Overripe fruit can be crushed/whizzed and sieved into juice to use in the basic recipe. You can combine fruits or have one fruit as jelly and another fruit as whole additions. Nice combinations are strawberry jelly/raspberries; blackcurrant jelly/blueberries; apple jelly/pear pieces; and so on. Note that pineapple and kiwi fruit stop jellies from setting properly, so avoid them, unless it is for decoration. We have suggested powdered gelatin, rather than leaf, as it is easier to use and to find in shops or online. Don't forget that you can get vegan gelatin substitute instead.

NOTE: if you decide to use gelatine leaves, or sachets of powdered gelatine, rather than spoonfuls from a tub, then the general rule is: Two gelatin leaves are equivalent to 1 teaspoon of powdered gelatin and a 11-12g sachet of powder is equivalent to 4 leaves of gelatin (therefore 2 teaspoons of gelatin from a tub).

BASIC JELLY RECIPE INGREDIENTS

- 1 pint (600mls) fruit juice (sieved to remove seeds and pulp. This will make a cloudy jelly. Alternatively, you could use some diluted cordial. See page 4) • 8ozs (200g) white sugar
- 8ozs (200g) frozen berries • 1 tablespoon or one sachet of gelatin powder

How to make:

1. In a medium saucepan, place 1 pint (600mls) juice and the sugar. Bring it to the boil. Remove from heat and whisk in gelatin until it dissolves.
2. Put several frozen berries in the bottom of individual serving dishes, then pour over the cooling jelly mixture. Refrigerate for 3-4 hours, or overnight, to set.
3. Decorate the set jellies with whipped cream and more berries.

JELLIES WITH ALCOHOL

There are two variations of this. One is making a larger jelly dessert with wine and the other is the fashion for jelly shots – jelly cubes with vodka or some other spirit.

JELLY SHOTS *(Keep away from children!)*

Ingredients

- 4 fl ozs (120ml) cold water • 4 fl ozs (120 mls) vodka or gin • 5 teaspoons gelatin
- 5 teaspoons of berry powder (see page 102)
- 8 fl ozs (640ml) boiling water

How to make:

1. Combine the cold water and the alcohol in a large bowl.
2. In a separate bowl or jug, combine the boiling water with the gelatin and berry powder. Stir well.
3. Add the cold water and alcohol mix to the flavoured jelly mix. Stir for a minute or two, then pour into ice cube trays, shot glasses or small chocolate moulds. Leave in the fridge overnight to set.
4. Serve with a warning that the shots contain alcohol!

JELLY DESSERT WITH PROSECCO

Ingredients

- 1lb (450g) fruit of your choice
- 8ozs (200g) caster sugar
- 5fl ozs (160ml) water
- 25fl ozs (750ml) prosecco (cold)
- 3 teaspoons of powdered gelatin

How to make:

1. Put prepared fruit, water and sugar in a heavy bottomed pan and heat until the sugar is dissolved and the mixture is boiling. Turn the heat down and let the mixture bubble for about 5 minutes, to achieve a colourful syrup.
2. Strain the mixture through a sieve into a bowl and leave it to drip. That way you will achieve a clear jelly. When it appears to have stopped dripping, discard the cooked fruit and, whilst the syrup is still hot, sprinkle the powdered gelatin over the bowl and stir in thoroughly.
3. Mix the cold prosecco with the fruit and gelatin syrup, then pour it into individual glasses and refrigerate overnight.
4. Decorate as you wish.

A Mousse by Any Other Name...

Posset, fool, mousse, trifle, syllabub, cream...purists will say that they are all different and, yet, they have one thing in common – they are all creamy dessert treats, easily made with the fruits from your garden. So, here, we are giving you a couple of basic creamy dessert bases, to which you can add fresh fruit, berry powders, fruit syrups or cordials. It's up to you. For a dairy free alternative, just replace cream, milk and yoghurt with plant-based alternatives. Coconut cream has become very popular for a rich dessert, as has silken tofu.

A MOUSSE BASE

Ingredients

- A 6ozs (150g) cold can of evaporated milk • ½pt (300ml) of berry jelly made from your choice of juice and 1 tablespoon of gelatin powder • 8ozs (200g) of washed berries of your choice

How to make:

1. Make the jelly, with the hot juice and gelatin powder. (See page 122). Leave to cool.
2. Whisk or process the evaporated milk until it is thick.
3. Add the cooled jelly to the whisked evaporated milk and continue whisking. It should increase in size.
4. Gently fold in the berries and dish out into one large serving dish or several individual dishes.
5. Refrigerate for a few hours. Decorate as you wish.

A FOOL BASE

Ingredients

- 8ozs (200g) prepared fruit (any fruit but preferably a sharp flavour) • 1 glass of white wine or diluted elderflower cordial • 1 tablespoon of honey • ¼pt (150ml) double cream

How to make:

1. Wash and prepare the fruit (remove any stalks, seeds or stones and cut up if necessary).
2. Cook the fruit in the wine or cordial and honey until it is a thick syrup, like jam. Leave it to cool.
3. Whip the cream until it forms stiff peaks.
4. Gently fold the whipped cream into the cooled fruit puree.
5. Spoon into individual glasses and refrigerate.
6. Decorate as you wish.

Meringues

If you have an oven that can be set low enough (some fan ovens just won't play ball!), then you can make meringues. And they are the most wonderful bases for absolutely any fruit and cream or ice cream, or even crushed up and mixed with fruit and ice cream to make what is known as a "Mess". Individual meringues are great party treats. You can make perfectly white meringues with white caster sugar, or if you want golden-coloured ones, then use fine brown sugar. When you put a large or individual meringues in the oven, just make a slight hollow in the centre of the mixture, so that you can add fruit and cream when you serve them.

Ingredients

- 3 egg whites • 6ozs (150g) fine white caster sugar • 1 tsp cornflour • 1 tsp vanilla essence

How to make:

1. Line a baking tray with greaseproof paper.
2. Pre-heat the oven to 140C (275F Gas Mark 1).
3. Beat the egg whites in a food processor until very stiff, then carefully and slowly, continue beating whilst adding the other ingredients.
4. Using a silicon spatula or large serving spoon, pile the meringue mixture on to the lined baking tray in either a large circle (dinner plate size) or small, well-spaced circles. Whatever the size, they need to be at least 1inch((2.5cms) thick with a depression in the middle.
5. Bake on the low heat setting for at least an hour or until the meringues are slightly golden and firm to the touch.
6. Remove the tray from the oven and leave it, and the meringues, to cool.
7. When cool, fill with whipped cream and fruit or, if serving immediately, then ice cream and fruit.

More publications by Iris Books that you may like...

IRIS BOOKS

The 100 Year Old School Cookbook

ISBN 978-1-907147-69-2

Compiled from genuine domestic science class textbooks. Amazing selection of household tips and recipes that were undertaken by 10 to 14 year olds at school during the period 1900 to 1920. A wonderfully nostalgic piece of social history. Beautifully illustrated.

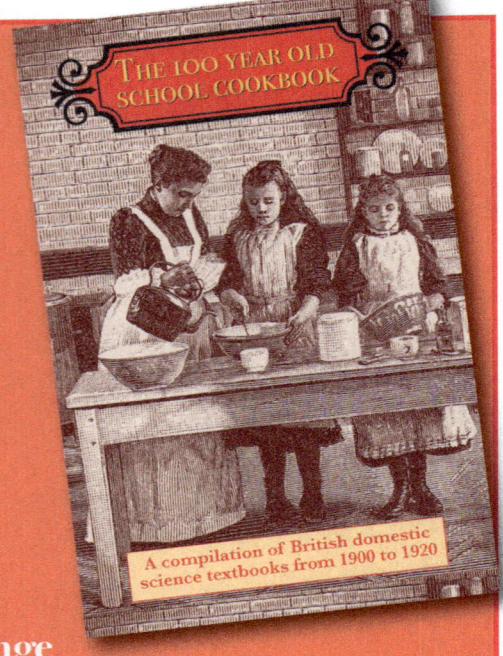

A compilation of British domestic science textbooks from 1900 to 1920

Cook's Advent Challenge

ISBN 978-1-907147-57-9

Laid out like a calendar, this joyously festive publication sets you the challenge of cooking a recipe every day of Advent. The recipes are from around the world, mark special days, internationally, in December, and provide lots of ideas for foodie gifts for your friends and family.

The books shown here are available from www.irisbooks.co.uk, in printed or Kindle format via Amazon, and through other online retail outlets.

Printed in Great Britain
by Amazon